I Want Chocolate Cake and I Want It Now!

CATHY GUISEWITE is a cartoonist whose work is popular all over the world. Her books include *Thin Thighs in Thirty Years*; *A Mouthful of Breath Mints and No One to Kiss*; *Men Should Come with Instruction Booklets*; and *The Child Within Has Been Awakened But The Old Lady on The Outside Just Collapsed*.

BARBARA ALBRIGHT is a registered dietitian, former editor-in-chief of *Chocolatier Magazine* and author of numerous cookery books.

I Want Chocolate Cake and I Want It Now!
Cathy's Cookbook for the Well-Balanced Woman

Cathy Guisewite
and
Barbara Albright

Thorsons
An Imprint of HarperCollins*Publishers*

Thorsons
An Imprint of HarperCollins*Publishers*
77–85 Fulham Palace Road,
Hammersmith, London W6 8JB

First published in the USA by Andrews McMeel Publishing
as *Girl Food: Cathy's Cookbook for the Well-Balanced Woman* 1997
Published in the UK by Thorsons 1998
3 5 7 9 10 8 6 4 2

A catalogue record for this book is
available from the British Library

ISBN 0 7225 3732 8

Printed in Great Britain by
Woolnough Bookbinding, Irthlingborough, Northants.

Great care has been taken to ensure that the information contained in this book is
accurate as at the date of publication. However, it is recommended that any readers
who suffer from a food allergy, or any other medical condition which may be affected
by diet, always seek the advice of a qualified medical practitioner for individual advice
before using any of the information in this book. No responsibility can be accepted by
the publishers or the authors for any loss, injury or damage caused by reliance upon
the accuracy of the information contained in this book or the use or misuse thereof.

Contents

Introduction

This is the cookbook that speaks to women.
Women who want romance.
Women who need chocolate.
Women who dream of wearing a swimsuit somewhere
other than the bathroom.
Women who need to entertain like sophisticated grown-ups.
Women who want to lie on the sofa in pyjamas and eat
chocolate cake.
In short, women whose lives are a little too complex to
have only one sort of recipe on hand at any given moment.

Here in one book, each woman will find a voice.
Each woman within each woman will find a recipe.
And every one of us can raise a fork, triumphant in the
knowledge that even if the world doesn't quite understand us,
at least there's a cookbook that does.

Romance Food

Romance Food

I once spent £90 preparing a romantic chicken dinner for a man: £30 in phone calls to girlfriends asking what I should make, £15 in phone calls to my mother asking how to make it, £30 to my therapist asking why I was making it, £10 for the saucepan, and £5 for the chicken.

What will work? That's all we really want to know, isn't it?

What will catapult me from 'dinner companion' to 'Irresistible Goddess' the fastest?

What will make him instantly oblivious to a few excess pounds, a few extra wrinkles, and/or the fact that prior to this evening, I didn't actually know how to cook anything that didn't have microwave instructions written on the side?

What will lure him away from sport on TV, and the World Wide Web?

And most important, what will I do to sustain the fantasy if meal number one works as planned and he can't wait to taste what I have in mind for meal number two?

After Commiserating with Twelve of My Closest Girlfriends, We've Decided He Really Loves Me
Apricot Walnut Muffins

These muffins go together very quickly. You can also substitute an equal quantity of other ingredients (such as chocolate chips, other dried fruits, and nuts) for the apricots and walnuts.

285g/10 oz plain flour

115g/4 oz brown sugar

2 teaspoons baking powder

1/4 teaspoon salt

200ml/7 fl oz milk

115g/4 oz unsalted butter, melted and cooled

1 large egg, lightly beaten

2 teaspoons vanilla essence

115g/4 oz chopped walnuts

200g/7 oz chopped dried apricots

Preheat the oven to 200°C/Gas Mark 6. Grease 12 7 x 3.5cm (3 x 1 1/4 inch) muffin tins or a 12-hole muffin tin.

In a large bowl, stir together the flour, brown sugar, baking powder, and salt. In another bowl, stir together the milk, butter, egg and vanilla until blended. Make a well in the centre of the dry ingredients. Add the milk mixture and stir just to blend. Stir in the walnuts and apricots to combine.

Spoon the batter evenly among the prepared muffin tins. Bake for 15 to 20 minutes, or until a skewer inserted into the centre of one muffin comes out clean and the muffins are just starting to brown.

Remove the muffin tin or tins to a wire rack. Cool for 5 minutes before removing the muffins; finish cooling on the rack. Serve warm or cool completely and store in an airtight container at room temperature.

Makes 12 muffins.

While He Casually Reads the Morning Paper, I'll Be Silently Planning Out the Course of Our Entire Relationship **Waffles**

To add a hint of citrus to these waffles, stir in 1/4 to 1/2 teaspoon of grated fresh orange or lemon zest. For romantic appeal, make these in a heart-shaped waffle iron. Serve with a salad made from seasonal fruits. If you don't use all the batter, it can be covered and refrigerated and used the next day.

285g/10 oz plain flour

55g/2 oz granulated sugar

1 1/4 teaspoons baking powder

1 teaspoon bicarbonate of soda

1 teaspoon salt

340ml/12 fl oz buttermilk, at room temperature

115g/4 oz unsalted butter, melted and cooled

2 large eggs, at room temperature, separated

2 teaspoons vanilla essence

Preheat the waffle iron according the manufacturer's instructions. (The iron is ready when a few drops of water sprinkled onto the surface immediately turn into dancing droplets.)

In a large bowl, stir together the flour, sugar, baking powder, bicarbonate of soda, and salt. In another bowl, stir together the buttermilk, butter, egg yolks, and vanilla. Make a well in the centre of the flour mixture. Add the liquid ingredients and stir just to combine.

In a grease-free medium-sized bowl, using an electric mixer set at medium-high speed, beat the egg whites until they just start to form stiff peaks when the beaters are lifted.

Using a rubber spatula, fold one-third of the beaten egg whites into the batter to lighten it. Fold in the remaining egg whites.

Pour the mixture into the centre of the preheated waffle iron, filling it about two-thirds full. Cook the waffles for 3 to 5 minutes, or until they are set (steam will stop coming out from the edges). Transfer the waffles to a warm oven and continue making the waffles until all the batter is used. Serve immediately.

Makes about 8 waffles.

The Less Time I Spend Making Breakfast, the More Time I Can Spend on My Makeup
Quick Crumb-Topped Banana Cake

Here's an easy cake that will use up ripe bananas. If you have bananas that are ripe, but don't have time to cook with them straight away, peel and store them in an airtight container in the freezer for up to three months. Let them thaw before mashing and using in recipes.

Crumb Topping:

70g/2^1/2 oz plain flour

55g/2 oz brown sugar

^{1}/4 teaspoon ground cinnamon

55g/2 oz unsalted butter, chilled and cut into 1 cm/^{1}/2 inch cubes

Banana Cake:

285g/10 oz plain flour

1^1/2 teaspoons baking powder

^{1}/2 teaspoon bicarbonate of soda

^{1}/2 teaspoon salt

2 medium size ripe bananas, mashed

90ml/3 fl oz milk, at room temperature

2 teaspoons vanilla essence

115g/4 oz unsalted butter, at room temperature

200g/7 oz granulated sugar

2 large eggs, at room temperature

Preheat the oven to 180°C/350°F/Gas Mark 4. Butter a 23cm/9-inch square or round baking tin.

To make the crumb topping:
In a medium bowl, stir together the flour, brown sugar, and cinnamon. Add the butter cubes. Using your fingertips, quickly rub the butter into the flour mixture until the mixture resembles small peas. Set aside.

To make the banana cake:
In a medium bowl, stir together the flour, baking powder, bicarbonate of soda, and salt. In another medium bowl, stir together the bananas, milk, and vanilla. In a large bowl, using a hand-held electric mixer, cream together the butter and sugar until blended. One at a time, add the eggs, beating well after each addition. In three additions each, alternately beat in the flour mixture and the banana mixture, until just combined.

Scrape the batter into the prepared tin, smoothing the surface with a spatula. Sprinkle the top evenly with the crumb topping. Bake for 40 to 45 minutes, or until a skewer inserted into the centre of the cake comes out clean and the cake is lightly browned.

Transfer the cake to a wire rack and cool. Serve warm.

Makes 9 servings.

Instead of Using the Old PVC skirt and Stiletto Heels Approach to Spice Things Up, I Think I'll Try Some Aphrodisiac Asparagus Vinaigrette

Asparagus is purported to have aphrodisiacal properties. In fact, in nineteenth-century France the bridegroom's prenuptial dinner was supposed to contain three courses of asparagus! Served on a bed of lettuce, this salad first course can be made ahead of time to provide an elegant beginning to any meal. As for asparagus's seductive powers, it's worth a try!

1 bunch of asparagus (about 565g/1 1/4 lb)

120ml/4 fl oz water

1/2 teaspoon salt

240ml/8 fl oz Basic Vinaigrette (recipe follows)

Lettuce leaves (optional)

Hold each stalk of asparagus and bend to snap off the tough base portion. If the asparagus are especially tough, peel the stalks with a vegetable peeler. Wash the asparagus in water, rinsing well so that no grit remains.

In a large saucepan, bring the water and salt to a boil. Add the asparagus, cover, and simmer for 6 to 8 minutes, or until the asparagus are crisp-tender. Drain the asparagus well and place them in a large shallow bowl. Add the Basic Vinaigrette, cover, and refrigerate for up to 24 hours, tossing occasionally to coat with the vinaigrette. Serve on a bed of lettuce, if desired.

Makes 4 servings.

Basic Romance Vinaigrette

Classic vinaigrette recipes use a ratio of three parts oil to one part vinegar. In this recipe we've used less oil, resulting in a tangier vinaigrette. If it is too tangy for your liking, increase the oil. Decrease the oil if you want it to be tangier. This basic recipe also lends itself to many variations. If you have fresh herbs, chop them up and add them to the dressing. In addition to being perfect for tossing with fresh salad ingredients (buy the ready-washed variety if you are in a hurry), vinaigrette is also delicious as a marinade for grilled meat, chicken, fish or vegetables.

200ml/7 fl oz vegetable oil

60ml/2 fl oz olive oil

140ml/5 fl oz red wine vinegar

1 tablespoon Dijon-style mustard

1 tablespoon freshly squeezed lemon juice

1 teaspoon dried basil leaves, crushed

1 medium garlic clove, cut in half

1/4 teaspoon dried oregano leaves, crushed

1/4 teaspoon dried thyme leaves, crushed

1/2 teaspoon salt

Dash of freshly ground pepper

Dash of Tabasco pepper sauce

In a large screw-top jar or a small bowl, shake or whisk together all of the ingredients. Remove the garlic halves before using the dressing. Refrigerate leftover dressing.

Makes about 425ml/3/4 pint dressing.

He Actually Believed Me When I Said I Could Cook Seduction Steak with Mushroom Sauce

When it comes to appealing to a man, sometimes it pays to go for the beef. Let him do the manly grilling and you take care of the sauce. Just like the two of you, this steak is a perfect partner with Parmesan Sun-Dried Tomato Potatoes (page 21).

Mushroom Sauce:

1 tablespoon butter

225g/8 oz sliced mushrooms

30g/1 oz chopped shallots

1/4 teaspoon salt

Dash of freshly ground black pepper

240ml/8 fl oz beef stock or broth

60ml/2 fl oz dry red wine

Steaks:

2 tender steaks (such as porterhouse or sirloin), each cut about 4cm/1 1/2 inch thick.

Salt and pepper to taste

To make the mushroom sauce:
In a medium saucepan, melt the butter over medium heat. Add the mushrooms, shallots, salt, and pepper. Cook for about 5 minutes, stirring occasionally. Add the broth and wine. Increase the heat to high and continue cooking until the mixture has been reduced by half.

To cook the steaks:
Preheat the grill. Position the grill pan approximately 10cm/4 inches from the heat source. Grill the steaks for 4 to 10 minutes on each side, depending on how well you like your steaks cooked. Season with salt and pepper. Serve with the mushroom sauce.

Makes 2 servings.

Cupid Is Alive and Well and Living in My Kitchen **Corn-fed Chicken**

1 corn-fed chicken (about 680g/1 1/4 lb)

1/2 teaspoon salt

1 tablespoon melted butter, divided

3 tablespoons good quality apricot jam

1 tablespoon Dijon-style mustard

Fruit and Nut Pilaf (page 18)

Preheat the oven to 200°C/400°F/Gas Mark 6. Wash and pat dry the chicken and sprinkle the inside with half the salt. Place the chicken, breast side up, on a rack set in a shallow roasting or baking tin. Brush with half of the butter. Roast for 30 minutes. Brush the chicken with the remaining half of the butter. Roast for 30 minutes longer.

Meanwhile, in a small saucepan, melt the apricot jam over a low heat. Stir in the mustard to combine and remove the pan from the heat. Brush the chicken with the glaze and roast about 30 minutes longer, or until the chicken is golden brown and the juices run clear when pierced with a fork. Serve with Fruit and Nut Pilaf.

Makes 2 servings.

Love Means Never Having to Say, 'Of Course I Like Football' Pork Tenderloin

This tenderloin is seasoned with an Asian-style marinade. The leftover marinade is cooked to form a delicious sauce. Serve it with rice and some steamed crisp-tender vegetables.

3 tablespoons tamari sauce (see Note)

1 tablespoon oriental-style sesame oil

1 tablespoon Dijon-style mustard

1 tablespoon finely chopped ginger root

1 spring onion, finely chopped (including the tender green tops)

1 medium garlic clove, finely chopped

1/8 teaspoon Tabasco pepper sauce

1 whole pork tenderloin (about 455g/1 lb)

120ml/4 fl oz chicken broth or stock

1 teaspoon cornflour

In a large bowl, stir together the tamari, sesame oil, mustard, ginger root, spring onion, garlic, and pepper sauce. Add the pork tenderloin and turn to coat with the marinade mixture. Refrigerate for at least 2 hours, turning the tenderloin occasionally.

Preheat the grill. Position the grill pan approximately 15cm/6 inches from the heat source. Place the tenderloin on the grill pan. Grill the tenderloin for about 10 minutes, turn and grill the other side for 10 minutes more, or until the tenderloin is completely cooked through. (It will register 160°F on a meat thermometer.)

Meanwhile, add the remaining marinade mixture to a small saucepan. Stir the broth and cornflour together to combine and add this to the marinade mixture. Cook over high heat and let the mixture boil for 1 minute, stirring constantly, until the sauce has thickened slightly. Slice the cooked tenderloin and serve with the sauce.

Makes 2 to 3 servings.

Note: Tamari sauce is a traditional Japanese soy seasoning available in the Asian section of grocery stores or in supermarkets.

If the Way to His Heart is Through His Stomach, This Will Be a Direct Hit Fruit and Nut Pilaf

2 teaspoons butter, divided

30g/1 oz chopped onion

115g/4 oz long-grain white rice

240ml/8 fl oz chicken broth or stock

Salt to taste

1/8 teaspoon freshly ground pepper

30g/1 oz pine nuts

55g/2 oz chopped dried apricots

In a medium saucepan, melt 1 teaspoon of the butter over medium heat. Add the onion and cook for about 5 minutes, or until softened. Add the rice and cook, stirring constantly, for 2 to 3 minutes, or until opaque. Add the chicken broth or stock, salt, and pepper. Increase the heat to high and bring the mixture to a boil, stirring occasionally. Cover the pan, reduce the heat to low, and simmer for 18 to 20 minutes, or until the rice has absorbed all the liquid.

In another small saucepan, melt the remaining teaspoon of butter over a medium heat. Add the pine nuts and cook for 2 minutes, or until the nuts are lightly browned. Stir the nuts and apricots into the rice mixture. Heat through.

Makes 2 to 3 servings.

This Will Make Him Forget He Ever Saw Me on a Bad Hair Day Pasta Puttanesca

This classic Italian pasta sauce is named after the *puttane* – the Italian ladies of the night. Its bold and lusty flavour is sure to make this a favourite in your kitchen when you want good eating. Serve it with an equally bold red wine, a tossed green salad, and a crusty loaf of bread to complete this feast.

170g/6 oz linguine or spaghetti

2 teaspoons olive oil

1 medium garlic clove, finely chopped

2 x 400g/14 oz tins plum tomatoes, drained and chopped

55g/2 oz black olives, stoned and sliced

1 tablespoon capers, drained

2 anchovy fillets, drained and mashed

1/2 teaspoon dried basil leaves, crushed

1/8 teaspoon dried oregano leaves, crushed

Pinch of crushed red pepper flakes

Salt and freshly ground pepper to taste

Chopped Italian flat or curly leaf parsley (optional)

Grated Parmesan cheese (optional)

Cook the pasta until *al dente*.

Meanwhile, in a large saucepan, heat the oil over medium heat. Add the garlic and cook for about 1 minute, or until the garlic has softened slightly. Add the drained tomatoes, olives, capers, anchovies, basil, oregano, and crushed red pepper flakes. Bring the mixture to a boil, stirring occasionally. Reduce the heat and simmer for about 15 minutes. Season with salt and pepper. Serve over the cooked pasta. Sprinkle with parsley and grated cheese, if desired.

Makes 2 generous servings.

AACK! He Found a Photo of Me When I Was 13
Salmon Potato Don't Fret Frittata

Delicious for breakfast, lunch, or dinner – or even for a very early morning breakfast after the party – a frittata is an Italian omelette that is cooked on both sides. Use this recipe as a basic frittata for creating your own varieties.

1 tablespoon olive oil

1 tablespoon butter

1 medium potato, scrubbed and cut into 1.5cm/1/2-inch cubes

1 spring onion, finely chopped (including tender green tops)

4 large eggs

55g/2 oz smoked salmon, cut into slivers

Salt and freshly ground pepper to taste

In a 20cm/8-inch frying pan, heat the oil and butter over medium heat. Add the potato cubes and cook, stirring occasionally, for 15 to 20 minutes, or until the potatoes are tender. Add the spring onion and cook 1 minute longer. If your frying pan does not have an ovenproof handle, wrap it with a double thickness of tin foil to protect it.

Meanwhile, in a medium bowl, whisk together the eggs, salmon, salt, and pepper just until combined. Position the grill pan so it is about 15cm/6 inches from the heat source. Preheat the grill.

Add the egg mixture to the frying pan with the potato mixture. Stir gently just until it begins to set. Then place the pan under the grill for 1 to 2 minutes, or until the egg mixture puffs and starts to brown lightly. Cut the frittata into wedges to serve.

Makes 2 servings.

Extremely Passionate
Parmesan Sun-Dried Tomato Potatoes

These twice-baked potatoes are full of flavour, filled with a delicious mixture that includes Parmesan cheese, sun-dried tomatoes and spring onions. Heat the milk in your microwave oven in a microwave-safe measuring jug. While you are preparing these, stuff more potatoes to enjoy another day. Cover and refrigerate the additional potatoes until you are ready to reheat them.

2 large potatoes

90–120ml/3–4 fl oz hot milk

2 tablespoons butter, softened

1/2 teaspoon salt

Pinch of freshly ground pepper

2 tablespoons sun-dried tomatoes in oil, drained and chopped

2 tablespoons spring onions, finely chopped (including tender green tops)

1 tablespoon grated Parmesan cheese

Preheat the oven to 220°C/425°F/Gas Mark 7. Scrub the potatoes well and then pierce them almost to the centre with a fork (this will allow steam to escape and it will keep the potatoes from bursting during baking). Place the potatoes directly on the oven rack and bake for about 1 hour, or until tender. Remove the potatoes from the oven and position the rack about 5 inches away from the grill and preheat.

Cut a slice (about 5mm/1/4 inch) off the top of each potato lengthways. Using a metal spoon, carefully scoop the insides of the potatoes into a medium bowl. Add most of the milk, butter, salt, and pepper. Using a handheld electric mixer, beat the potato mixture until smooth, adding additional hot milk if necessary. Add the tomatoes, spring onions and Parmesan cheese and beat just until combined.

Spoon the mixture into the potato shells. Place the potatoes on the grill pan and grill for 1 to 2 minutes, or until the tops are lightly browned.

Makes 2 servings.

Even Though He's Sound Asleep on the Sofa, I Know He'll Protect Me Hero Sandwich

This hearty man-sized sandwich is layered with cheese and meat and then smothered with a delicious cooked vegetable mixture. It is a perfect sandwich for a picnic or barbecue.

2 tablespoons olive oil

1 small onion, thinly sliced

1 garlic clove, finely chopped

1 small aubergine, thinly sliced

1 medium courgette, thinly sliced

1 small tomato, thinly sliced

1/2 red or green pepper, seeded and thinly sliced

55g/2 oz sliced mushrooms

2 tablespoons red wine vinegar

1/2 teaspoon dried basil leaves, crushed

1/4 teaspoon dried oregano leaves, crushed

1/4 teaspoon salt

Dash of freshly ground pepper

1 loaf Italian or French bread (about 225g/8 oz)

340g/12 oz total of your favourite thinly sliced luncheon meats and cheeses (such as salami, provolone, Cheddar, smoked ham or turkey)

2 tablespoons grated Parmesan cheese

In a large frying pan, heat the oil over medium-high heat. Add the onion and garlic and cook for about 5 minutes, or until softened slightly. Add the aubergine, courgette, tomato, pepper, mushrooms, vinegar, basil, oregano, salt and pepper. Simmer for 15 to 20 minutes, or until the vegetables are softened and most of the liquid has evaporated, stirring the mixture occasionally. Remove the pan from the heat and cool.

Slice the loaf of bread in half lengthways and scoop out most of the soft insides. Line each side of the loaf with the meats and cheeses. Evenly distribute the vegetables over the meats and cheeses. Sprinkle the surface with the Parmesan cheese. Place the halves of the sandwich together. Wrap in foil or clingfilm. Unwrap the loaf and use a serrated knife to cut the sandwich into slices.

Makes 2 very generous servings.

Would You Like to Stop by the Jewellers on the Way to the Rugby Match Chocolate Chip Brownies

Chocolate speaks the language of love. These dense rich brownies are speckled with chocolate chips. They are perfect for picnics, and to send to him when he's out of town. You can also use a square of these brownies as the base for a brownie sundae. Top it with a scoop of ice cream, drizzle with Hot Fudge Sauce (page 123), and add a dollop of whipped cream.

225g/8 oz unsalted butter

200g/7 oz plain chocolate, broken into pieces

4 large eggs, at room temperature

200g/7 oz granulated sugar

115g/4 oz brown sugar

1 tablespoon vanilla essence

140g/5 oz plain flour

1/4 teaspoon salt

255g/9 oz chocolate chips

115g/4 oz chopped walnuts or pecans (optional)

Preheat the oven to 180°C/350°F/Gas Mark 4. Line a 32 x 2cm/13 x 9 inch baking tin with tin foil so that the foil extends 5cm/2 inches beyond the two long sides of the tin. Lightly grease the bottom and sides of the foil-lined tin.

In a large microwave-safe bowl, heat the butter and chocolate in a microwave oven on high for 1 to 3 minutes, stirring halfway through cooking, until the chocolate is melted (or place the bowl in a pan of hot, not simmering, water). Let it stand at room temperature for 20 minutes.

In a large bowl, using a handheld electric mixer set at medium-high speed, beat the eggs and sugars for 2 to 3 minutes, or until the mixture is light in colour. Beat in the chocolate mixture and vanilla until blended. Beat in the flour and salt just until combined. Using a wooden spoon, stir in the chocolate chips and the nuts, if using.

Scrape the batter into the prepared pan and spread evenly. Bake for 30 to 40 minutes, or until a skewer inserted into the centre comes out with fudgy crumbs. Cool the brownies in the tin set on a wire rack. Cut into rectangles.

These brownies freeze well.

Makes 20 brownies.

After Five Hundred and Two Dinners and Four Hundred and Twenty-Seven Cups of Coffee, I Think It's Time to Get Serious Marry Me Mousse

This decadent mousse uses raspberry-flavoured liqueur. Serve it in stemmed dessert glasses or wineglasses and garnish each serving with a few raspberries and a sprig of mint or a dollop of whipped cream and a few chocolate curls. Try the recipe with other flavours of liqueur such as orange-flavoured liqueur or cognac.

255g/9 oz plain chocolate, broken into pieces

120ml/4 fl oz milk

A few grains of salt

1 tablespoon vegetable oil

1 tablespoon black raspberry liqueur (such as Chambord)

1 1/2 teaspoons vanilla essence

240ml/8 fl oz double or whipping cream, chilled

In the bowl of a food processor fitted with a metal chopping blade, process the chocolate for 20 to 30 seconds, or until it is finely chopped.

In a small saucepan, over medium heat, cook the milk and salt, until the mixture just comes to a boil. Stirring occasionally with a wooden spoon. Remove the pan from the heat.

With the motor of the food processor running, pour the hot milk through the feed tube. Process for 10 to 20 seconds, or until the chocolate is completely melted. Add the oil, liqueur, and vanilla and process for 5 to 10 seconds longer, or until the mixture is combined. Scrape the mixture into a large bowl and let stand for 20 to 30 minutes, or until cool.

In a chilled large bowl, using a handheld electric mixer with chilled beaters, beat the cream until peaks just start to form.

Using a rubber spatula, gently fold one-third of the whipped cream into the chocolate mixture to lighten it. Fold in the remaining whipped cream just until combined.

Spoon the mixture into four stemmed dessert glasses or wineglasses. Cover the glasses with clingfilm and refrigerate for 1 to 2 hours, or until the mixture is set. The mousse may be prepared up to 2 days in advance.

Makes 4 servings.

He'll Keep Coming Back for More
Amore Amaretto Cheesecake

Cream-filled chocolate sandwich biscuits form the easy crust for this decadent chocolate-swirled cheesecake. If you have a food processor, process the biscuits using a metal chopping blade until they are crushed. Add the melted butter and process about 30 seconds longer or until the mixture is combined.

Biscuit Crust:

16 cream-filled chocolate sandwich biscuits, crushed into crumbs

2 tablespoons unsalted butter, melted

Chocolate-Swirled Amaretto Cheesecake Filling:

2 cartons (225g/8 oz each) cream cheese, softened

200g/7 oz granulated sugar

1 tablespoon plain flour

3 large eggs, at room temperature

120ml/4 fl oz sour cream, at room temperature

60ml/2 fl oz amaretto

1 teaspoon vanilla essence

55g/2 oz chocolate, melted and cooled

To make the biscuit crust:
Preheat the oven to 170°C/325°F/Gas Mark 3. Lightly butter the bottom and side of a 20cm/8-inch springform tin. Place the tin on a piece of tin foil and press it to cover the

bottom and part of the side to prevent any batter from leaking out.

In a bowl, stir together the crushed biscuits and butter. Using your fingers, press the mixture firmly and evenly onto the bottom and 2 cm/^{3}/$_4$ inch up the side of the tin.

To make the filling:
In a large bowl, using a handheld electric mixer, beat the cream cheese until just smooth. Beat in the sugar and flour. Beat in the eggs one at a time. Using a wooden spoon, stir in the sour cream, amaretto and vanilla.

Scrape all but 3 tablespoons of the batter into the prepared pan. In a small bowl, stir together the reserved batter and the melted chocolate until combined.

Pour the chocolate in 1.5cm/^{1}/$_2$ inch-wide parallel lines, about 3cm/1 inch apart, on top of the filling. Insert the tip of a small knife about 1.5cm/^{1}/$_2$ inch deep into the filling. Working perpendicular to the chocolate strips, draw the knife back and forth in lines to create a feathery marbled effect.

Bake for 45 to 55 minutes, or until the centre of the cheesecake is set and it is just beginning to brown around the edge. Turn off the oven and open the door slightly. Let the cheesecake stand in the oven for 30 minutes longer. Remove the cake to a wire rack and cool completely.

Cover the top of the springform tin tightly with clingfilm and refrigerate overnight, or for at least 4 hours, until well chilled. Take the cheesecake from the refrigerator 30 minutes before serving and remove the side of the springform tin. Cut the cheesecake into wedges with a sharp, thin knife.

Makes about 10 servings.

Swimsuit Food

Swimsuit Food

Nothing compels me toward 'sensible eating' like getting a good look at my winter body in a summer mirror. Okay, fine, maybe I should have taken a peek before 1 June. Perhaps it was a mistake to wear baggy long skirts with elastic waistbands for the past six months. Possibly the swimwear manufacturers aren't entirely to blame.

Still, I feel I've suffered enough just by walking into the swimwear department. I shouldn't also have to deprive myself of food.

Besides, the body is in natural harmony with the changing of the seasons and since mid-March has been belligerently rejecting anything that hints of 'low-fat'.

It's not just time for action. It's time for trickery. Fool the fat cells into thinking they're getting a nice, big breakfast. Fool the stomach into thinking it's had a full-calorie lunch. Fool the thighs into believing they're getting chocolate cake.

Look this fat-free, reduced-calorie, boring world in the eye, say 'HAH!' and then march into the kitchen and make something that's guiltless *and* good to eat.

And for once make the words 'active lifestyle' mean something more than standing in the changing room ripping a ten-inch piece of lycra to shreds.

It's Monday and I'm Motivated
Low-Fat Bran Muffins

Here's a muffin recipe with a minimum amount of fat. Its moist texture is a result of using plain yogurt and apple sauce.

170g/6 oz bran cereal (such as All-Bran)

240ml/8 fl oz low-fat natural yogurt

140ml/5 fl oz chunky apple sauce

120ml/4 fl oz skimmed milk

225g/8 oz plain flour

1 teaspoon ground cinnamon

1 teaspoon baking powder

1 teaspoon bicarbonate of soda

1/4 teaspoon salt

2 large eggs

2 tablespoons molasses

1 tablespoon vegetable oil

1 teaspoon vanilla essence

55g/2 oz brown sugar

Preheat the oven to 200°C/400°F/Gas Mark 6. Grease 12 7 x 3.5cm (3 x $1/4$ inch) muffin tins or a 12-hole muffin tin.

In a large bowl stir together the cereal, yogurt, apple sauce, and skimmed milk. Let the mixture stand until the liquid is absorbed. Meanwhile assemble the remaining ingredients.

In a large bowl, stir together the flour, cinnamon, baking powder, bicarbonate of soda, and salt.

In another large bowl, stir together the eggs, molasses, oil and vanilla until combined. Stir in the brown sugar. Stir in the bran mixture until combined. Make a well in the centre of the flour mixture and stir in the egg–bran mixture just to combine.

Spoon the batter evenly among the prepared muffin tins. Bake for 15 to 20 minutes, or until a skewer inserted into the centre of one muffin comes out clean.

Remove the muffin tin or tins to a wire rack. Cool for 5 minutes before removing the muffins from the tins; finish cooling on the rack. Serve warm or cool completely and store in an airtight container at cool room temperature.

These muffins freeze well.

Makes 12 muffins.

I Don't Want to Go Shopping; I Have to Eat Healthy; What's in the Fridge
Vegetable Omelette for One

One of the easiest and most satisfying meals is an omelette. A plain omelette is terrific on its own, but often your refrigerator holds the makings for some delicious fillings or toppings, either savoury or sweet. A vegetable filling has fewer calories than one that includes cheese. A hot-cheese omelette, however, could provide a feeling of satisfaction and keep you from snacking later on. Because the actual omelette cooks very quickly, prepare the filling before you are ready to fill the omelette. To keep the eggs hot when you serve them, run your plate under hot water to take off the chill and dry it before you top it with your freshly cooked hot omelette.

Basic Omelette:

2 large eggs

2 tablespoons water

$1/8$ teaspoon salt

Dash of freshly ground pepper

2 teaspoons unsalted butter

In a small bowl, whisk together the eggs, water, salt and pepper until blended.

In a 20cm/8 inch nonstick frying pan, cook the butter over medium-high heat until it is just starting to sizzle. Pour in the egg mixture. (The egg mixture will begin to set immediately around the edge.) Carefully push the cooked portions at the edge toward the centre, allowing the uncooked mixture to flow toward the surface of the pan. Tilt the pan and move the cooked portions as necessary so that the omelette is completely cooked. If you are filling the omelette, add the filling while the top is still moist and creamy-looking. Using a spatula, fold the omelette in half or fold two sides in toward the centre. Invert the omelette onto the plate with a quick flip of the wrist or slide the omelette from the pan onto a plate.

Makes 1 serving.

Filling possibilities:

You can create your own filling with one or two ingredients. If you want to flavour the egg part itself, mix about $1/8$ to $1/4$ teaspoon of your favourite herb or spice into the egg mixture. You can use some raw vegetables and fruits as a filling, but to give the omelette a more finished flavour, sauté the vegetables and fruit in a small amount of butter in the omelette pan until they are tender. (You can also steam them.) Set them aside, cook the omelette, and then return them to the omelette.

To get you started, here are some ideas:

Apple and Blue Cheese – Sauté half a sliced small green apple in 2 teaspoons of butter until the apple is tender. Fill the almost cooked omelette with the cooked apple and 2 tablespoons of crumbled blue cheese and fold the omelette.

Herbed Brie – Add about $1/4$ teaspoon total of dried thyme, basil, oregano, marjoram or dill weed to the egg mixture. To the almost cooked omelette, add a slice or two of Brie and fold the omelette.

Ham and Cheese – Sprinkle the almost cooked omelette with 30g/1 oz of finely chopped cooked ham and 30g/1 oz of grated cheese and fold.

Broccoli and Cheese – Sprinkle the almost cooked omelette with about 55g/2 oz cooked broccoli florets and 30g/1 oz grated cheese and fold.

Omelette Olé – Top the almost cooked omelette with 90ml/3 fl oz salsa sauce and 55g/2 oz grated Cheddar cheese and fold the omelette. Spoon a tablespoon of low-fat sour cream on top.

Pizza – Add about $1/4$ teaspoon of dried oregano to the egg mixture. Top the almost cooked omelette with 4 tablespoons tomato sauce, 30g/1 oz grated mozzarella cheese, and 2 tablespoons of cooked mushrooms and fold.

Always a Bridesmaid … Never the Same Size
Low-Calorie Coleslaw

This coleslaw is made with a yogurt and reduced-calorie mayonnaise dressing. If you have any peppers, cut them into thin strips and add them to the slaw.

240ml/8 fl oz natural yogurt

3 tablespoons reduced-calorie mayonnaise

1/4 teaspoon salt

1/8 teaspoon Tabasco pepper sauce

115g/4 oz thinly sliced or chopped green cabbage

115g/4 oz thinly sliced or chopped red cabbage

170g/6 oz grated carrot

In a large bowl, stir together the yogurt, mayonnaise, salt, and Tabasco sauce. Add the cabbages and carrot and toss gently to combine all the ingredients. Can be served chilled or at room temperature. Cover and refrigerate any leftovers.

Makes about 4 servings.

At the First Sign of Autumn, the Dreaded Slinky Hipsters Search Begins **Easy Black Bean Soup**

Canned beans make this soup (souper easy) extra easy. Add less broth if you want a thicker soup. Serve it with a crusty wholegrain bread and a tossed green salad.

2 teaspoons olive oil

55g/2 oz chopped onion

55g/2 oz chopped green pepper

1 medium garlic clove, finely chopped

$1/2$ teaspoon ground cumin

425g/15 oz tin black beans, drained

1 395g/14 oz tin reduced-salt chicken broth or stock

Salt and freshly ground pepper to taste

Chopped tomatoes and/or reduced-fat sour cream (optional)

In a medium saucepan over medium heat, heat the oil. Add the onion, green pepper, garlic, and cumin and cook, stirring frequently, for 5 to 7 minutes, or until the vegetables are softened. Add the beans and chicken broth and cook until heated through. Season with salt and pepper. Serve in warmed bowls or mugs topped with chopped tomatoes and/or reduced-fat sour cream, if desired.

Makes 2 servings.

Who Needs a Five-Pound Box of Chocolate When You Have **A Really Big Salad**

When you are looking for quantity and not calories, here's a jumbo salad to try. Substitute your own favourite vegetables or select those that look the best at the market. Top with sliced grilled chicken, canned water-packed drained tuna, drained beans, or a sliced hard-boiled egg to add extra substance to the salad. Serve it with any of the following homemade salad dressings or use your favourite brand of reduced-calorie dressing. To make it easier and to avoid waste, select just the right amount of ingredients at a supermarket salad bar; top your creation with one of the following dressings.

170g/6 oz torn lettuce leaves

55g/2 oz spinach leaves

6 cherry tomatoes, cut in half

6 mushrooms, rinsed and sliced

1 small carrot, grated

1/2 small cucumber, sliced

1/2 small red onion, chopped

In a large bowl, gently toss all the ingredients. Drizzle with one of the following salad dressings and serve.

Makes 1 jumbo serving.

Skinny Dilled Dijon Yogurt Dressing

Use the basic mixture of yogurt and mayonnaise as the foundation for other flavours of dressings. This makes a fabulous dip for raw vegetables. For a thinner dressing, stir in a little skimmed milk until you achieve the consistency you desire.

90ml/3 fl oz low-fat natural yogurt

90ml/3 fl oz reduced-calorie mayonnaise

15g/1/2 oz chopped fresh parsley

2 tablespoons chopped fresh dill

2 teaspoons Dijon-style mustard

Salt and freshly ground black pepper to taste

In a medium bowl, whisk together the yogurt, mayonnaise, parsley, dill and mustard until combined. Season with salt and pepper. Cover and refrigerate the dressing until you are ready to serve it.

Makes just under 240ml/8 fl oz dressing.

Svelte Chinese Dressing

Add strips of grilled chicken, bean sprouts, and mandarin oranges to A Really Big Salad (page 40) along with this dressing to turn it into A Really Big Chinese Chicken Salad.

120ml/4 fl oz rice vinegar

3 tablespoons soy sauce

1 1/2 tablespoons finely chopped fresh ginger

1 tablespoon granulated sugar

1 tablespoon Dijon-style mustard

1 tablespoon oriental-style sesame oil

1 small garlic clove, finely chopped

Dash of Tabasco pepper sauce

In a small container with a cover that fits tightly, combine all of the ingredients and shake to mix. Cover and refrigerate the dressing until you are ready to serve it.

Makes just under 240ml/8 fl oz dressing.

Creamy Thin Goddess Salad Dressing and Dip

Here's a thick dressing/dip that tastes substantial even though its calories are minimal. Serve it with crudités for weight watchers. It's also superb on top of baked potatoes.

15g/^{1}/2 oz fresh parsley leaves

15g/^{1}/2 oz fresh basil leaves

225g/8 oz low-fat cottage cheese

2 tablespoons reduced-calorie mayonnaise

Freshly ground black pepper to taste

In the container of a blender or food processor fitted with a metal chopping blade, process the parsley and basil until finely chopped. Add the cottage cheese and mayonnaise and continue to process until the mixture is smooth. Season with pepper. Cover and refrigerate the dressing until you are ready to serve.

Makes about 285ml/^{1}/2 pint dressing.

'Tis Better to Be Fit Than to Be Fried
Three-Ingredient Unfried Chicken

This chicken stays moist because of its yogurt and breadcrumb coating. Be extra virtuous and remove the skin of the chicken before you bake it. Bake a potato at the same time you cook the chicken. As it all bakes, munch on a few raw veggies. Serve it with a tossed salad or Low-Calorie Coleslaw (page 38).

One (0.9–1.3kg/2–3 lb) chicken, cut up into 8 pieces

240ml/8 fl oz natural yogurt

115g/4 oz Italian-seasoned dry breadcrumbs

Preheat the oven to 190°C/375°F/Gas Mark 5. If desired, remove the chicken's skin. Place the yogurt in a shallow bowl. Place the breadcrumbs in a shallow plate.

Roll each piece of chicken first in the yogurt and then in the breadcrumbs. Place the coated pieces of chicken in a baking tin. Bake for about 1 hour, or until the juices run clear when the chicken is pricked with a fork.

Makes 4 to 6 servings.

My Jeans Have Shrunk and Now So Must I
Tex-Mex-Style Rice, Black Bean, Sweetcorn and Pepper Salad

Here's a satisfying colourful salad that is packed with fibre. A lime-juice-and-coriander-based dressing adds lively flavour to the salad. It is great for storing in a plastic container for lunch. Serve it on a platter lined with lettuce leaves as perfect party food.

90ml/3 fl oz freshly squeezed lime juice

1 tablespoon olive oil

1/4 teaspoon Tabasco pepper sauce

1/4 teaspoon salt

340g/12 oz cooked brown rice

1 tin (425g/15 oz) black beans, drained and rinsed

200g/7 oz cooked sweetcorn

115g/4 oz chopped red pepper

115g/4 oz chopped yellow pepper

30g/1 oz chopped spring onions

15g/1/2 oz chopped coriander

1 jalapeño pepper, seeded and finely chopped

In a large bowl, stir together the lime juice, olive oil, Tabasco sauce and salt. Add the rice, beans, sweetcorn, red pepper, yellow pepper, spring onions, coriander and jalapeño pepper and toss gently to coat.

Makes about 4 servings.

Nothing Encourages Revenge Like A School Reunion **Slim Fries**

Here's a potato recipe that looks and tastes like the deep-fat fried variety. When you first get home from work, scrub the potatoes, slice them into 1.5cm/1/2 inch wide strips, toss them into iced water, and preheat the oven. Then get changed and read the post before popping the potato strips into the oven.

2 medium potatoes, unpeeled, scrubbed and trimmed of any bruised spots

2 teaspoons butter, melted (in the microwave oven)

Salt and freshly ground pepper to taste

Slice the potatoes lengthways into 1.5cm/ 1/2 inch thick strips. Place the strips of potatoes in a bowl of iced water for 20 minutes.

Meanwhile, preheat the oven to 230°C/ 450°F/Gas Mark 8. Spray a baking sheet with nonstick vegetable or olive oil cooking spray. Drain the potatoes thoroughly and dry on paper towels.

Place the potatoes in a single layer on the prepared baking sheet. Brush with half of

the melted butter. Bake for 20 minutes. Turn the potatoes, brush with the remaining butter and bake for 20 minutes longer, or until lightly browned. Sprinkle with salt and pepper.

Makes 1 large serving.

Why Did I Buy a Itsy-Bitsy Teeny-Weeny Bikini Linguine

Here's a pasta that's easy on the thighs. This recipe serves two. If it is just you eating, immediately put half of the mixture into an airtight container and refrigerate it to reheat and enjoy the next day. For a few extra calories, sprinkle a little grated Parmesan cheese on top.

115g/4 oz thin linguine

1 tablespoon olive oil

55g/2 oz chopped onion

1 medium garlic clove, finely chopped

Pinch of crushed red pepper flakes

1/4 teaspoon dried basil leaves, crushed

90ml/3 fl oz dry white wine

1 tin (170g/6 oz) minced clams, undrained

3 tablespoons chopped fresh parsley

Salt and freshly ground black pepper to taste

Cook the linguine according to the instructions on the packet and drain thoroughly.

Meanwhile, in a large frying pan, heat the oil over medium heat. Add the onion, garlic, pepper flakes and basil and cook, stirring frequently, for 4 to 6 minutes, or until the vegetables are tender.

Add the wine, increase the heat, and bring the mixture to a boil. Boil until about half of the liquid has evaporated. Add the clams and their liquid and continue cooking for about 2 to 3 minutes, or until heated through. Stir in the parsley. Add the drained linguine to the frying pan and toss to coat with the clam mixture. Season with salt and pepper and serve.

Makes 2 servings.

AACK! He Wants to Go Tropical
Thin Thighs Turkey

This fresh-tasting recipe has captured the taste of Thailand using readily available ingredients. Use packaged turkey breast fillets for the turkey. You can also use chicken breasts.

200ml/7 fl oz chicken broth

3 tablespoons chopped spring onions (including tender green tops)

2 tablespoons chopped coriander leaves

2 tablespoons soy sauce

1 tablespoon freshly squeezed lime juice

2 teaspoons cornflour

2 teaspoons oriental-style sesame oil

225g/8 oz turkey breast, cut into strips (5cm x 5mm/2 x 1/4 inch)

1/4 teaspoon crushed red pepper flakes

1 medium red pepper, seeded and cut into strips (5cm x 5mm/2 x 1/4 inch) (about 115g/4 oz)

225g/8 oz hot cooked rice

In a small bowl, stir together the chicken broth, spring onions, coriander, soy sauce, lime juice and cornflour and set aside.

In a nonstick wok or large frying pan, heat the sesame oil over medium-high heat. Add the turkey and crushed red pepper flakes and cook, stirring constantly, for 2 to 3 minutes. Add the red pepper and cook for 2 minutes. Stir the chicken broth mixture and add it to the wok. Bring the mixture to a boil and cook for 1 minute to thicken the sauce. Serve with the cooked rice.

Makes 2 servings.

Now That I've Committed to a Slinky Black Dress, I Have to Lose Ten Pounds Balsamic Dijon Marinated Steak

This easy marinade is full of flavour and can be used with other types of meat and poultry. Try it with pork chops. We recommend marinating the steak in a plastic bag as it takes up less room in the refrigerator. Of course, you can always allow the steak to stand in the marinade in a glass bowl.

200ml/7 fl oz balsamic vinegar

2 tablespoons olive oil

2 tablespoons Dijon-style mustard

2 garlic cloves, finely chopped

1 teaspoon dried basil leaves, crushed

1/4 teaspoon Tabasco pepper sauce

Steak (0.45–1.3kg/1–3 lb)

In a large freezer-weight plastic bag (or use two ordinary plastic bags, one inside the other), combine the vinegar, oil, mustard, garlic, basil and pepper sauce. Add the steak and seal the bag. 'Squish' the bag so that the mixture completely covers the steak. Place the bag in the refrigerator for 8 hours or overnight, occasionally turning the bag to distribute the marinade.

Position the grill pan about 13cm/5 inches from the heat source. Remove the steak from the marinade. Grill the steak for 4 to 8 minutes on each side, or until cooked to the desired degree. If desired, brush the steak with the remaining marinade as it cooks. Thinly slice the steak diagonally across the grain.

Makes 4 to 6 servings.

In This Fast-Paced World of Greasy Take-Away Food, You Have to Stop and Smell the **Lean Burgers**

When nothing but a burger will do, here is a slimmed-down version that combines lean ground beef and ground turkey breast. Cook the number of burgers you need for dinner and individually wrap the rest of the burgers and freeze them for another day.

455g/1 lb ground lean beef

455g/1 lb ground turkey breast

225g/8 oz chopped onions

2 tablespoons Worcester sauce

3/4 teaspoon dried thyme leaves, crushed

1/4 teaspoon dried oregano leaves, crushed

1/2 teaspoon salt

1/4 teaspoon freshly ground pepper

85g/3 oz thinly sliced low-fat mozzarella or other low-fat cheese

6 hamburger buns

6 lettuce leaves

6 slices of tomato

Position the grill pan about 13cm/5 inches from the heat source.

In a large bowl, using a wooden spoon or your hands, mix together the beef, turkey, onions, Worcester sauce, thyme, oregano, salt and pepper until combined. Shape the mixture into 6 patties.

Grill the burgers for 5 to 7 minutes on each side or until cooked completely through. Top the burgers with the cheese and continue cooking about 30 seconds, or until the cheese melts. Place the burgers on the buns. Top with the lettuce and tomato and serve.

Makes 6 burgers.

I'm Invited to a Beach Party and I'd Rather Not Have to Wear a Tent Grilled Tuna with Papaya Salsa

Use this marinade and salsa with chicken or other types of fish, too!

Tuna:

2 tablespoons freshly squeezed lime juice

1 teaspoon olive oil

1 small garlic clove, finely chopped

Dash of salt and freshly ground pepper

1 tuna steak, 3–4cm/1–1$1/2$ inches thick (about 115–170g/4–6 oz)

Papaya Salsa:

1 ripe papaya, peeled, seeded and chopped

$1/2$ medium red pepper, seeded and chopped

30g/1 oz chopped red onion

15g/$1/2$ oz chopped coriander leaves

4 tablespoons freshly squeezed lime juice

$1/2$ small jalapeño pepper, seeded and finely chopped

$1/4$ teaspoon salt

To marinate the tuna:
In a shallow dish, combine the lime juice, oil, garlic, salt and pepper. Add the tuna steak and turn to coat it with the marinade. Cover and refrigerate it for up to 2 hours, or until you are ready to cook the tuna.

To make the papaya salsa:
Meanwhile, in a medium bowl, gently toss together all of the salsa ingredients to combine. Cover and refrigerate the salsa until you are ready to use it.

To grill the tuna:
Position the grill pan about 13cm/5 inches from the heat source. Grill the tuna steak for about 4 to 6 minutes on each side. Serve with the salsa. Refrigerate any leftover salsa to use another time.

Makes 1 serving plus extra salsa.

Just Because I'm Healthy Doesn't Mean I Have to Suffer Low-Calorie Chocolate Sauce

A spoonful of this rich-tasting chocolate sauce will jazz up almost any dessert. Try it spooned over sliced bananas, strawberries or Chocolate Angel Cake (page 56) for a low-fat dessert. Use a flavoured liqueur, such as Grand Marnier, in place of the vanilla for extra flavour. For espresso flavour, stir in a pinch of instant espresso powder.

30g/1 oz cocoa powder

55g/2 oz brown sugar

2 teaspoons cornflour

240ml/8 fl oz water

1 1/2 teaspoons vanilla essence

In a medium saucepan, stir together the cocoa powder, brown sugar, and cornflour until combined. Stir in the water and heat over medium-high heat, stirring constantly, until the mixture comes to the boil. Boil for 1 minute to thicken the sauce. Stir in the vanilla. Cover and refrigerate any leftovers.

Makes 340ml/12 fl oz sauce.

I Refuse to be Victimized by the Gene Pool Fat-Free Chocolate Angel Cake

This moist and lofty cake is flavoured with espresso and cocoa powder. Serve it with fresh fruit and a spoonful of vanilla yogurt for a low-calorie dessert that tastes decadent!

140g/5 oz plain flour

30g/1 oz cocoa powder

225g/8 oz granulated sugar

1 teaspoon instant espresso powder

1/4 teaspoon salt

12 large egg whites, at room temperature

1 teaspoon cream of tartar

2 teaspoons vanilla essence

1 tablespoon icing sugar for sifting over the cake

Position a rack in the bottom third of the oven and preheat the oven to 180°C/350°F/Gas Mark 4.

In a medium bowl, stir together the flour, cocoa powder, 85g/3 oz granulated sugar, espresso powder and salt. Sift the mixture onto a piece of waxed paper

In a grease-free, large bowl, using a handheld electric mixer set at medium speed, beat the egg whites for 20 to 30 seconds, or until foamy. Beat in the cream of tartar. Gradually increase the speed to high and continue beating until soft peaks start to form. Beat in the vanilla. Two tablespoons at a time, beat in the remaining granulated sugar. In three additions, sift the flour/cocoa mixture over the surface of the beaten egg whites, and using a rubber spatula, gently fold in each addition just until combined.

Scrape the batter into a grease-free 23cm/9 inch ring mould and gently smooth the surface. With a long knife, cut through the batter to remove any large air bubbles. Bake for 40 to 50 minutes, or until the top is dry and it springs back when touched lightly with your fingertip.

Invert the cake to cool. Cool for about 1 1/2 hours. Loosen the cake with a metal spatula and invert it onto a serving plate. Sift the icing sugar evenly over the cake.

Makes 12 servings.

Slob-Out Food

Slob-Out Food

Men take a taste and leave the rest. Women take a taste and eat the whole pie. Men date. Women turn it into a relationship. It's as simple as that.

For all their pre-match bags of crisps and sandwiches, men will never truly understand one of the most nurturing, cosy, happy concepts of life: food as companion.

Not to be confused with revenge food or self-pity food, Slob-Out Food is simply what we need to eat sometimes when we just want to curl up with a good friend, but don't necessarily want another human being in the room.

This is food you could be proud to serve to company sometime, but will be positively delirious to serve to yourself anytime.

It's a vacation from stress, a time-out from the diet, the 'I'm worth it, I deserve it, I-don't-want-to-talk-about-it-just-let-me-eat' kind of food you pray will be waiting for you in your refrigerator every time you open the door.

And, needless to say, it's all the more delicious when you eat it while lying on the sofa wearing clothes designed for intense exercise.

Turn Out the Lights, Pop in a Video, and Pass the Bowl Parmesan Popcorn

A simple sprinkling of Parmesan cheese on popcorn turns it into an extra-special salty snack! Make your favourite type of popcorn – homemade or microwave – and adjust the amount of Parmesan according to the saltiness of the popcorn and your personal taste. (The cheese will not stick as well to air-popped or nonfat popcorn.)

Enough popcorn for 2 people

15–30g/½–1 oz grated Parmesan cheese, to taste

In a large bowl, toss together the popcorn and the Parmesan cheese to combine.

Makes 2 servings.

I Need the Afternoon to Rearrange My Wardrobe and Make Room for the New Clothes I Plan to Purchase Sassy Salsa Guacamole

If you want to speed up the ripening of your avocado, place it in a paper bag for a few days.

1 medium-size ripe avocado, skin and stone removed

3 medium-size ripe tomatoes, finely chopped

30g/1 oz chopped spring onions (including tender green tops)

3 tablespoons chopped coriander

1 medium serrano or other hot chilli pepper, trimmed, seeded, and finely chopped

2 tablespoons freshly squeezed lime juice

1 garlic clove, crushed

1/2 teaspoon salt

In a medium bowl, mash the avocado. Stir in the tomatoes, spring onions, coriander, pepper, lime, garlic and salt. Cover. Chill until ready to serve. Serve with crisps, cut-up fresh vegetables, or Toasted Parmesan Pitta Triangles (page 87).

Makes just over 570ml/1 pint dip.

This is the Perfect Evening to Lock Ourselves In and Try on All Our Makeup Samples Crab Cakes with Red Pepper Tartare Sauce

These crab cakes are substantial enough to be a main course, yet they could also be used as a first course. Try them served in a roll as a delicious 'burger'.

Crab Cakes:

455g/1 lb crabmeat, well picked over (or use frozen, thawed, and drained crab)

2 large eggs, lightly beaten

2 tablespoons mayonnaise

2 tablespoons chopped fresh parsley

2 tablespoons chopped spring onions (including tender green tops)

1 tablespoon freshly squeezed lemon juice

1/4 teaspoon salt

1/4 teaspoon Tabasco sauce

115g/4 oz crackers, crushed

1 to 2 tablespoons olive oil

1 to 2 tablespoons unsalted butter

Red Pepper Tartare Sauce:

115g/4 oz finely chopped red pepper

30g/1 oz finely chopped spring onions (including tender green tops)

120ml/4 fl oz mayonnaise

120ml/4 fl oz sour cream

1 tablespoon freshly squeezed lemon juice

1 tablespoon chopped fresh parsley

Generous dash of Tabasco pepper sauce

To make the crab cakes:
In a large bowl, gently stir together the crab, eggs, mayonnaise, parsley, spring onions, lemon juice, salt and pepper sauce. Stir in the crushed crackers.

Form the mixture into about six cakes that are each about 10cm/4 inches across and about 2cm/³/₄ inch thick.

In a large frying pan, heat 1 tablespoon of the oil and 1 tablespoon of the butter over medium-high heat. Add as many crab cakes as will fit and cook for 3 to 5 minutes on each side or until they are lightly browned and cooked through. Repeat until all the crab cakes are cooked. Add additional oil and butter as necessary to keep the crab cakes from sticking. Drain well on paper towels.

To make the red pepper tartare sauce:
Meanwhile, in a medium bowl, stir together all of the tartar sauce ingredients until combined. Cover and refrigerate until ready to serve.

Makes 6 crab cakes and about 425ml/³/₄ pint sauce.

I'm Having My Own Little Fiesta at Home **Enchiladas**

This is a loose adaptation of a true enchilada that captures all the craved-for flavours of old Mexico – easily! If you have extra cooked chicken or beef, add it to the filling of this enchilada. Try it with Sassy Salsa Guacamole (page 63).

115g/4 oz refried beans

240ml/8 fl oz picante sauce

1 tablespoon chopped drained bottled jalapeño peppers

1 tablespoon chopped spring onions (including tender green tops)

1/4 teaspoon ground cumin

One 25cm/10-inch diameter flour tortilla

115g/4 oz grated Cheddar cheese

85g/3 oz shredded lettuce

85g/3 oz chopped tomatoes

Sour cream for garnish (optional)

Preheat the oven to 180°C/350°F/Gas Mark 4. In a small bowl, stir together the beans, 4 tablespoons of the picante sauce, jalapeños, spring onions, and cumin until combined.

Place the tortilla on a work surface. Place the bean mixture down the centre of the tortilla. Top the mixture with half of the cheese. Roll the sides of the tortilla over the filling and place the filled enchilada in a small baking dish (a loaf tin works well), seam side down.

Spoon the remaining picante sauce over the enchilada. Sprinkle with the remaining cheese. Bake for 20 to 25 minutes, or until heated through. Remove enchilada from the oven and transfer to a plate. Smother the enchilada with the lettuce and tomatoes. Garnish with sour cream, if desired.

Makes 1 serving.

Swimsuits Are Way Overrated **Boboli Olé**

Use ready-made bases to make pizza in a flash. Here's one that combines popular Mexican-flavoured ingredients.

90ml/3 fl oz salsa sauce

One 15cm/6-inch pizza base

115g/4 oz grated Cheddar cheese

Preheat the oven to 230°C/450°F/Gas Mark 8.

Spread the salsa sauce evenly over the surface of the pizza base. Sprinkle the cheese over the salsa. Bake for 10 to 12 minutes, or until the pizza is heated through and the cheese is bubbly.

Makes 1 serving.

I Need Some Quality Time with My Dog
Sky-High Scone-Crusted Pizza

Here's an easy pizza with a crust that is simply leavened with baking powder. Chopped walnuts and wholewheat flour make the base extra interesting. We've topped this pie with broccoli, roasted red peppers, and goat cheese along with traditional mozzarella cheese, which gives this pie its towering proportions. Of course, you can also use your favourite pizza toppings.

Dough:

115g/4 oz wholewheat flour

115g/4 oz plain flour

3 tablespoons finely chopped walnuts

1 1/2 teaspoons baking powder

1/8 teaspoon salt

55g/2 oz unsalted butter, chilled and cut into cubes

4 tablespoons milk

1 large egg

Topping:

2 teaspoons olive oil

1/2 teaspoon dried basil leaves, crushed

1/4 teaspoon dried oregano leaves, crushed

1 (285g/10 oz) pack thawed frozen broccoli florets, drained

55g/2 oz strips of homemade or drained bottled roasted red peppers (see Note)

115g/4 oz goat cheese, cut into 1.5cm/1/2 inch pieces

30g/1 oz coarsely broken walnuts

225g/8 oz grated mozzarella cheese

Preheat the oven to 200°C/400°F/Gas Mark 6. Lightly grease 28cm/11 inch diameter circle in the centre of a baking sheet or pizza tin.

In a large bowl, stir together the flours, chopped walnuts, baking powder and salt. Distribute the butter cubes evenly over the flour mixture. With your fingertips, quickly press the butter and flour mixture together until the mixture resembles coarse crumbs. In a small bowl, stir together the milk and egg. Add the liquid mixture to the dry ingredients and stir to combine until the mixture pulls together.

With lightly floured hands, pat the dough into a 25cm/10-inch-diameter circle in the centre of the prepared baking sheet.

Brush the surface of the dough with the olive oil. Sprinkle the basil and oregano evenly over the top.

Evenly distribute the broccoli, red pepper strips, goat cheese, and broken walnuts over the surface. Sprinkle the mozzarella cheese over the top. Bake for 20 to 25 minutes, or until the cheese is melted and the crust is lightly browned.

Remove from the baking sheet to a wire rack. Cut the pizza into wedges and serve.

Makes 2 generous servings.

Note: To roast a pepper, position the grill pan 12 to 15cm/5 to 6 inches from the heat source. Preheat the grill. Grill the pepper, turning it, until the skin is lightly and evenly charred. When the pepper is cool, rub away the burnt skin. Stem and core the pepper.

I'd Go to the Gym but I Seem to Have Misplaced My Energy Artichoke Mushroom Tortellini Salad

Here's an easy recipe that's great for dinner one day and as lunch the next. Using marinated artichokes and their liquid for the dressing keeps this recipe extra easy. If the salad stands and needs more dressing, add a little olive oil and red wine vinegar. You can use other flavours of tortellini if that is what you have on hand.

225g/9 oz fresh, mushroom tortellini

1 jar (170g/6 oz) marinated artichoke hearts with liquid

2 tablespoons sun-dried tomatoes in oil, drained and sliced

115g/4 oz smoked turkey, cut into slivers

30g/1 oz stoned and sliced ripe olives

Grated Parmesan cheese (optional)

Cook the tortellini according to the instructions and drain thoroughly.

In a large bowl, gently toss together the hot tortellini, artichokes (with their liquid), tomatoes, turkey, and olives. Sprinkle with Parmesan cheese, if desired. This is good at room temperature or refrigerated. Cover and refrigerate leftovers.

Makes 2 servings.

It's Saturday Night and I'm Wearing My Dressing Gown Date Nut Scones

These moist scones are full of dates and nuts. Try chocolate chips and dried fruits in place of the dates and nuts for other variations.

2 large eggs, lightly beaten

120ml/4 fl oz buttermilk or milk

1 1/2 teaspoons vanilla essence

280g/10 oz plain flour

55g/2 oz granulated sugar

1 1/2 teaspoons baking powder

1/2 teaspoon bicarbonate of soda

1/4 teaspoon salt

85g/3 oz unsalted butter, chilled and cut into 1cm/1/2-inch cubes

140g/5 oz stoned, chopped dates

30g/1 oz chopped walnuts or pecans

Preheat the oven to 200°C/400°F/Gas Mark 6. Lightly grease a baking sheet.

Reserve 1 tablespoon of the egg for brushing on top of the scones. In a medium bowl, stir together the buttermilk, remaining eggs and vanilla.

In a large bowl, stir together the flour, sugar, baking powder, bicarbonate of soda and salt. With a pastry blender or two knives used scissors fashion, cut in the butter until the mixture resembles coarse crumbs. Stir the buttermilk mixture into the flour mixture until combined. Stir in the dates and nuts. Turn the dough out onto a lightly floured surface and knead it for 30 to 60 seconds, or until combined.

On the floured surface, pat the dough out into a 15cm/6-inch square. Cut the dough into 5cm/2-inch squares. Transfer the scones to the prepared baking sheet and brush the tops with the reserved egg. Bake for 14 to 17 minutes, or until the scones are lightly browned.

Transfer the baking sheet to a wire rack and cool for 5 minutes. Using a spatula, transfer the scones to the wire rack and cool. Serve warm.

Makes 9 scones.

I Love Workout Clothes … They Have Such Stretchy Wastebands Good Old-Fashioned Spaghetti and Meatballs

If you don't have the time or energy to make meatballs, the sauce is good all by itself over pasta.

Tomato Sauce:

1 tablespoon olive oil

115g/4 oz chopped onion

1 medium garlic clove, finely chopped

2 tins (400g/15 oz) Italian-style tomatoes, chopped, with their juice

1 tin (400g/15 oz) tomato sauce

4 tablespoons tomato purée

1 small bay leaf

1 teaspoon dried basil leaves, crushed

1/4 teaspoon dried oregano leaves, crushed

1/4 teaspoon salt

1/8 teaspoon freshly ground pepper

Meatballs:

455g/1 lb ground beef

55g/2 oz Italian-seasoned dry breadcrumbs

1 large egg, lightly beaten

2 medium garlic cloves, finely chopped

1/2 teaspoon salt

1/8 teaspoon freshly ground pepper

2 tablespoons olive oil

340g/12 oz spaghetti

To make the tomato sauce:
In a large saucepan, heat the olive oil over medium-high heat. Add the onion and garlic and cook for 7 to 10 minutes, stirring occasionally, until the onion is softened. Add the tomatoes and their juice, tomato sauce, tomato purée, bay leaf, basil, oregano, salt and pepper. Reduce the heat and simmer, stirring occasionally, for about 30 minutes.

To make the meatballs:
Meanwhile, in a large bowl, gently mix together the ground beef, breadcrumbs, egg, garlic, salt, and pepper until combined. Shape the mixture into about eighteen meatballs, using about 2 tablespoons of mixture for each one.

In a large frying pan, heat the oil over medium-high heat. Add the meatballs and cook for 4 to 6 minutes, turning to brown all the surfaces. With a slotted spoon, transfer the meatballs to paper towels to drain. Add the meatballs to the tomato sauce. Simmer gently for 15 minutes. Remove and discard the bay leaf from the sauce.

Meanwhile, cook the pasta according to the instructions on the packet and drain thoroughly. Add the meatballs and sauce to the spaghetti and serve.

Makes 6 servings.

The Four-and-a-Half-Hour, Five-Phone Call
Chocolate Chunk Cherry Almond Bread Pudding

It's easy to pick away at this entire dish – whether you are picking at the crusty top or going after a chewy cherry, a melting square of chocolate, or a toasted almond sliver …

5 large eggs

170g/6 oz brown sugar

0.7l/1 1/4 pints milk

1 tablespoon almond essence

1 loaf (about 285g/10 oz) Italian or French bread, cut into 2.5cm/1 inch cubes

170g/6 oz dried cherries

255g/9 oz plain chocolate, cut into 1 cm/1/2 inch pieces

55g/2 oz slivered almonds

Preheat the oven to 170°C/325°F/Gas Mark 3. Lightly grease a baking dish (33 x 23 x 5 cm/13 x 9 x 2 inches).

In a large bowl, whisk together the eggs until combined. Whisk in the brown sugar. Whisk in the milk and almond essence until blended.

Add the bread cubes and toss to moisten the cubes with the mixture. Gently stir in the cherries, chocolate and almonds. Scrape the mixture into the prepared dish. Bake for 45 to 50 minutes, or until the mixture is set. Serve warm. Cover and refrigerate any leftovers for up to five days. Reheat to serve.

Makes 8 to 10 servings.

I Woke Up Late Anyway So Why Bother Leaving the House Spiced Apple-Filled Coffee Cake

Here's a cake that's layered with a spicy streusel mixture. It's a natural with coffee at breakfast – actually for any time of the day. Serve it with a scoop of vanilla ice cream for dessert.

Streusel:

55g/2 oz plain flour

55g/2 oz brown sugar

1/2 teaspoon ground cinnamon

1/8 teaspoon ground cloves

1/8 teaspoon ground ginger

1/8 teaspoon ground nutmeg

3 tablespoons unsalted butter, chilled and cut into 1cm/1/2 inch cubes

115g/4 oz chopped pecans or walnuts

Apple Cake:

425g/15 oz plain flour

1 tablespoon baking powder

1/2 teaspoon salt

225g/8 oz unsalted butter, softened

285g/10 oz granulated sugar

4 large eggs, at room temperature

1 tablespoon vanilla essence

4 tablespoons milk, at room temperature

170g/6 oz coarsely grated tart apples (such as Granny Smith)

140g/5 oz raisins

Icing sugar for sifting over the top of the cake (optional)

To make the streusel:
In a medium bowl, stir together the flour, brown sugar, cinnamon, cloves, ginger and nutmeg. Add the butter cubes. Using your fingertips, quickly rub the butter into the flour mixture until the mixture resembles coarse crumbs. Stir in the nuts and set aside.

To make the apple cake:
Preheat the oven to 170°C/325°F/Gas Mark 3. Butter a 25cm/10-inch cake tin. Dust the tin with flour and tap out the excess.

In a medium bowl, stir together the flour, baking powder and salt. In a large bowl, using a handheld electric mixer, beat together the butter and sugar until combined. One at a time, beat in the eggs, beating well after each addition. Beat in the vanilla. In three additions each, alternately beat in the flour mixture and the milk, beating just until combined. Beat in the apples. Using a wooden spoon, stir in the raisins.

Sprinkle about one-third of the streusel evenly over the bottom of the prepared tin. Spoon half of the batter over the streusel and spread evenly. Sprinkle the batter evenly with another one-third of the streusel. Spoon the remaining batter over the streusel and spread evenly. Sprinkle the remaining one-third of the streusel evenly over the top. Bake for 65 to 75 minutes, or until a skewer inserted into the centre of the cake comes out clean and the cake is lightly golden.

Transfer the tin to a wire rack. Cool for 10 minutes. Carefully invert the cake onto the rack and cool completely. Sift icing sugar over the top of the cake, if desired. Store the cake in an airtight container at cool room temperature. Can be stored up to 5 days.

Laundry Night
Chocolate Chunk Macadamia Nut Cookies

When the laundry calls, the name of the game is sustenance and convenience. These decadent cookies fill the bill perfectly!

340g/12 oz plain flour

3/4 teaspoon baking powder

1/4 teaspoon salt

225g/8 oz unsalted butter, softened

170g/6 oz brown sugar

85g/3 oz granulated sugar

2 large eggs, at room temperature

2 teaspoons vanilla essence

340g/12 oz plain chocolate, broken into squares

170g/6 oz chopped lightly salted macadamia nuts

In a large bowl, stir together the flour, baking powder and salt. In another large bowl, using a wooden spoon, cream together the butter and sugars. One at a time, add the eggs to the butter–sugar mixture, stirring well after each addition. Stir in the vanilla. Gradually stir in the flour mixture until combined. Stir in the chocolate chunks and nuts. Cover and refrigerate the dough for at least 2 hours or overnight.

Preheat the oven to 150°C/300°F/Gas Mark 2. Using a 1/4-cup measuring cup, drop the dough by cupfuls onto an ungreased baking sheet, leaving at least 5cm/2 inches between the dough mounds. Bake one sheet at a time, for 30 to 35 minutes, or until the cookies are lightly browned. Remove the baking sheet to a wire rack and cool for 5 minutes. Using a metal spatula, transfer the cookies to wire racks and cool completely. Repeat until all the dough is used. When cool, store the cookies in an airtight container for up to 2 weeks.

These cookies freeze well for up to 3 months.

Makes about 22 cookies.

A Good Book, a Glass of Milk, and Thou Banana Bread

It seems that bananas are either too green or they've become a major attraction for flies. Here's an easy recipe for banana bread to use those bananas that are soft and speckled with brown spots.

225g/8 oz plain flour

1 teaspoon baking powder

1/2 teaspoon bicarbonate of soda

1/4 teaspoon salt

115g/4 oz unsalted butter, softened

170g/6 oz granulated sugar

2 large eggs, at room temperature

2 large bananas, mashed

3 tablespoons milk

2 teaspoons vanilla essence

55g/2 oz chopped walnuts or pecans (optional)

Preheat the oven to 180°C/350°F/Gas Mark 4. Lightly grease a loaf tin (22 x 11 1/2 x 6 cm/8 1/2 x 4 1/2 x 2 1/2 inches).

In a large bowl, stir together the flour, baking powder, bicarbonate of soda and salt. In another bowl, and using a wooden spoon, cream together the butter and sugar until blended. One at a time, add the eggs, beating well after each addition. Add the bananas, milk and vanilla and stir just until combined. (The mixture may look curdled.) Stir in the flour mixture just until blended. Stir in the nuts, if using.

Scrape the batter into the prepared tin and spread evenly. Bake for 45 to 55 minutes, or until a skewer inserted into the centre of the bread comes out clean and the bread is slightly browned.

Remove the tin to a wire rack. Cool for 10 minutes before removing the bread from the tin; finish cooling on the rack. Store the completely cooled bread in an airtight container at cool room temperature.

Makes 1 loaf; 12 to 16 slices.

Grown-Up Food

Grown-Up Food

Like many dynamic, successful women of my generation, I always fantasized that, one day, I would entertain groups of witty, intelligent friends in my home.

The day came and went and all I had to serve my guests was a half-eaten bag of crisps. 'Where's the food?' I wondered. 'Where are the chic hors d'oeuvres?' 'What sort of hostess would invite people into her home and make them root through the cupboards for their own refreshments??!'

It was only when I began arm-wrestling one of my guests for the last diet coke that I realized with horror that we were, in fact, in my home. That I was the hostess. And that, shockingly, it was my turn to be the grown-up.

If the fact that I was in charge wasn't frightening enough, it was immediately followed by the realization that even if I had thought to prepare something, I wouldn't have had the slightest idea what to make.

Armed with the following dishes, I have since learned that being the grown-up requires only a few basic ingredients:

1. a great recipe
2. a good attitude
3. lots of time left over to hide the dirty pans in the garage and obsess about your hair.

AACK! They're Coming in Twenty-Three Minutes **Red Pepper Dip/Spread**

This versatile and sophisticated concoction is superb as a speedy party dip but also works well as a topper for canapés. Trim the crust from slices of hearty wholegrain bread and spread each slice with a thick layer of spread. Cut each slice into quarters and then cut each quarter in half to form two triangles. If desired, decorate each piece with slivers of roasted red pepper, ripe olives or chives. For Valentine's Day, when entertaining that special someone, cut the bread into heart shapes using a metal cookie cutter. This rosy spread is also great as a sandwich spread on hearty wholegrain bread or a bagel.

4 tablespoons drained sun-dried tomatoes in oil, oil reserved

1 medium garlic clove, finely chopped

1 jar (200g/7oz) roasted red peppers, drained

3 to 5 drops Tabasco pepper sauce

1 carton (225g/8oz) cream cheese, softened

In a small frying pan or skillet, cook garlic in 2 teaspoons of the reserved oil for 2 to 4 minutes, or until the garlic is softened.

In the container of a food processor fitted with a metal chopping blade, process the tomatoes, garlic mixture, red peppers and pepper sauce until smooth (with small pieces of tomato remaining). Add the cheese and process with an on-and-off motion until the mixture is blended. Scrape the mixture into a small bowl and serve immediately with the Toasted Parmesan Pitta Triangles (page 87), crackers, crisps, and/or raw vegetable dippers. Cover and refrigerate any leftovers for up to 5 days.

Makes about 425ml/$^3/_4$ pint dip.

I'm Throwing a Party and Forgot to Plan a Menu
Toasted Parmesan Pitta Triangles

These breads are full of flavour and are a simple snack on their own but are delicious as 'dippers' for almost any kind of dip.

Pitta bread

Olive oil

Grated Parmesan cheese

Preheat the oven to 180°C/350°F/Gas Mark 4. Split each pitta bread horizontally into two rounds. Lightly brush the rough sides with olive oil. Sprinkle a thin layer of Parmesan cheese over the olive oil.

Cut each pitta round into wedges (the number depends on the diameter of pitta bread that you are using). Arrange the triangles on a baking sheet and bake for 5 to 10 minutes, or until lightly toasted. Serve with dips or as an accompaniment with soups and salads. Store leftover triangles in an airtight container at cool room temperature up to 5 days.

I Only Have Time for Half a Shower, One Coat of Nail Polish and Two Ingredients Party Brie

Here's a super easy party recipe. Place the plate that held the cheese while it was being heated in the centre of a larger platter. Surround it with small clusters of grapes or crackers and slices of French bread for an attractive presentation. Of course, you can scale this recipe down accordingly to work with a small wheel of Brie.

1 wheel (1 kg/ 4 lb) of Brie

1 small jar sun-dried tomatoes in oil,
    chopped and drained

Place the Brie on a microwave-safe plate large enough to hold the cheese and small enough to fit into your microwave oven. It's helpful if the plate has a rim. Using a sharp knife, trim off the top crust (about 1 cm/ $^1/4$ inch) from the cheese.

Scatter the chopped tomatoes evenly over the cut surface of the cheese. Cover the tomato-topped cheese with clingfilm and microwave on high for 2 to 4 minutes, or until the cheese is melted. Serve the cheese with crackers and slices of bread. If the cheese gets cool and firm, return it to the microwave oven and cook it for 1 to 2 minutes longer, or until it is soft again.

Makes 10 to 12 servings.

I've Invited Aunt Ethel … Lock Up the Photo Albums Tomato, Basil and Garlic Bruschetta

Here's a recipe that's well-suited to the summer when tomatoes and basil are at their very best. Serve it with a salad at the beginning of any meal to make a first impression that will last and last. Served with a salad, bruschetta also makes a simple casual meal if you grate a little cheese on top.

12 fresh ripe medium Italian plum tomatoes, finely diced

30g/1 oz fresh basil leaves, cut into thin strips

2 tablespoons finely chopped garlic

1 tablespoon red wine vinegar

Salt and freshly ground pepper to taste

4 tablespoons extra-virgin olive oil

1 loaf (26–30cm/10 to 12 inches long) of crusty country-style or French bread

In a large bowl, toss together the tomatoes, basil, 1 tablespoon of the garlic, vinegar, salt and pepper.

In a small frying pan or skillet, over medium heat, cook the olive oil and the remaining 1 tablespoon of garlic for 2 to 3 minutes, or until the garlic is just starting to brown. Remove from the heat.

Using a serrated knife, cut the bread into 2cm/3/4-inch thick slices. Lightly brush one side of each slice of bread with the garlic-infused oil. Position a grill pan about 15cm/6 inches from the heat source and grill the brushed side of the bread for 1 to 2 minutes, or until lightly browned. Turn the slices of bread and brush with the remaining oil. Grill for 1 to 2 minutes, or until lightly browned. Top each slice of bread with a generous spoonful of the tomato mixture.

Makes about 6 to 8 servings.

His Old Girlfriend Will be There ... I Hear She's Allergic to Cheese Quick Jalapeño Cheese Quesadilla with Tex-Mex Salsa

Use any leftover black beans from making the salsa to sprinkle over salads or as an ingredient in soup. Add chopped fresh spring onions and coriander for a livelier made-from-scratch taste.

Tex-Mex Salsa:

1 jar (310g/11 oz) tomato salsa

115g/4 oz frozen, thawed; or drained, canned sweetcorn

85g/3 oz drained rinsed black beans

2 spring onions (including tender green tops), finely chopped

15g/1/2 oz chopped coriander leaves

Jalapeño Cheese Quesadillas:

Four 25cm/10-inch flour tortillas

340g/12oz grated mature Cheddar cheese

8 tablespoons drained bottled sliced jalapeños

To make the Tex-Mex salsa:
In a large bowl, stir together the salsa, sweetcorn, beans, spring onions and coriander.

To make the jalapeño cheese quesadillas:
Preheat the oven to 230°C/450°F/Gas Mark 8.

Lightly brush both sides of each tortilla with water. Place one tortilla on a baking sheet. Top half of the tortilla with one quarter of the cheese and 2 tablespoons of the jalapeños. Fold the tortilla over to cover the filling. Repeat with the remaining ingredients.

Bake for 5 to 7 minutes, or until the quesadillas are lightly browned and the cheese is melted. Cut into wedges to serve. Serve with the Tex-Mex salsa.

Makes about 4 servings (425ml/3/4 pint salsa).

What Was I Thinking When I Said, 'Stop by Anytime', **Marvellous Mango Chutney Cheese Spread**

Here's a spread that has an intriguing medley of flavours that will have everyone returning to it again and again. It's best when allowed to come to room temperature. Leftovers make a delicious sandwich filling on a hearty wholegrain bread such as pumpernickel.

225g/8 oz cream cheese, softened

340g/12 oz grated mature Cheddar cheese

Few drops of Tabasco pepper sauce

1 jar (285g/10 oz) mango chutney, chopped

5 strips of bacon, cooked until crisp, drained and crumbled

6 spring onions (including tender green tops), chopped

In a medium bowl, using a fork, stir together the cream cheese, half the Cheddar cheese, and the Tabasco sauce until combined. Spread the mixture over a 20–25cm/8–10-inch serving dish, smoothing the surface evenly.

Spread the chutney over the surface. Sprinkle the chutney with the remaining Cheddar cheese, the bacon and the spring onions. Serve immediately with crackers or celery sticks. Cover and refrigerate any leftovers for up to two days.

Makes 8 to 10 servings.

Nothing Says Confidence Like Ooh la la Provençal Tapenade

This classic French spread is full of flavour and is wonderful on crackers and slices of French bread. Its deep dark colour looks great when served alongside Sassy Salsa Guacamole (page 63) and Red Pepper Dip/Spread (page 86). An alternative use is as an easy appetizer: scrub and cook small new potatoes until they are just tender. Cut the potatoes in half or into thick slices and spread a spoonful on top of each one.

1 tin (170g/6 oz drained weight) stoned ripe olives, drained

1 tin (55g/2 oz) anchovy fillets in olive oil, drained

2 tablespoons olive oil

1 tablespoon drained capers

1 tablespoon Dijon-style mustard

1 small garlic clove, coarsely chopped

Dash of Tabasco pepper sauce

Place all the ingredients in the container of a food processor fitted with a metal chopping blade. Process until the ingredients are combined, but still with a somewhat coarse texture, scraping down the side of the container with a rubber spatula if necessary. Scrape the spread into a small bowl. Serve immediately or cover and refrigerate to allow the flavours to blend. Can be served chilled or at room temperature.

Makes about 285ml/$1/2$ pint tapenade.

Since We're Only Having Brunch We Should Be Able to Eat Enough for the Two Other Meals We're Missing Italian Sausage Mushroom Strata

Here's a recipe that is perfect for brunch. You assemble it the day before and then simply pop it into the oven to bake, enabling you to be a guest at your own party. To complete the menu, serve an assortment of breads and muffins along with a fruit salad made with seasonal fruits.

455g/1 lb hot Italian sausage, casings removed

455g/1 lb mushrooms, sliced

2 medium onions, sliced

55g/2 oz sliced spring onions

3/4 loaf (600g/21 oz) Italian or French bread cut into 2.5cm/1 inch cubes

340g/12 oz grated mature Cheddar or other type of cheese

55g/2 oz freshly grated Parmesan cheese

12 large eggs, lightly beaten

scant 850ml/1 1/2 pints milk

3 tablespoons spicy brown mustard

1/4 teaspoon freshly ground black pepper

Lightly butter a large baking tin (approximately 43 x 25 x 5cm/15 x 10 x 2 inches).

In a large pan or frying pan, heat the sausage, mushrooms and onions for about 20 minutes, or until the sausage is cooked through and the vegetables are tender. Drain off the fat. Stir in the spring onions.

Arrange half of the bread cubes in the prepared baking tin. Spread half of the sausage–vegetable mixture over the bread cubes. Sprinkle half of the Cheddar cheese and half of the Parmesan cheese over the top. Repeat the layers.

In a large bowl, whisk together the eggs, milk, mustard and pepper. Pour the egg mixture evenly over the strata. Cover and refrigerate the strata overnight.

Preheat the oven to 180°C/350°F/Gas Mark 4. Bake for 50 to 60 minutes, or until the strata is puffed and golden and cooked through.

Makes 8 to 10 servings.

It's a Family Reunion and I Don't Know a Soul
Vegetarian Chilli

Here's a fresh-tasting chilli that you can easily assemble with your guests. Ask for help chopping the vegetables and toppings and you can have it ready in a flash. Serve ice cold beer as an accompaniment. Use kitchen scissors to cut the tinned tomatoes into pieces. Just stick the point of the scissors right down into the open tin and cut away until all the tomatoes are chopped. For bean lovers, add an extra tin of drained kidney beans. You can also use your favourite type of bean.

1 tablespoon vegetable oil

225g/8 oz chopped onions

2 medium green peppers, seeded and chopped

3 medium garlic cloves, finely chopped

3 medium jalapeño peppers, seeded and finely chopped (leave the seeds in for a hotter chilli)

3 tablespoons chilli powder

1 teaspoon dried oregano leaves, crushed

1/2 teaspoon salt plus additional salt to taste

4 tins (400g/14 oz) Italian-style plum tomatoes, chopped, with their juice

1 tin (170g/6 oz) tomato purée

1 tin (565g/20 oz) red kidney beans, drained

1 tin (425g/15 oz) pinto beans, drained

1 tin (425g/15 oz) chick peas, drained

225g/8 oz diced courgettes

Grated mature Cheddar cheese, sour cream, chopped onion or spring onion, chopped tomatoes or chopped olives for serving on top of the chilli (optional)

In a large heavy saucepan, heat the oil over medium heat. Add the onions, peppers, garlic and jalapeños. Cook for about 10 to 12 minutes, or until the vegetables are softened, stirring occasionally.

Stir in the chilli powder, oregano and salt. Add the tomatoes and their juice, tomato purée and beans. Simmer for 25 minutes, stirring occasionally. Add the courgettes and cook for 5 to 10 minutes, continuing to stir occasionally. Season with salt. Ladle into bowls and serve with the toppings, if desired.

Makes about 10 to 12 servings.

You Never Know When You'll Meet the Man of Your Dreams So Be Sure to Bring a Good Dish Marinated Vegetable Couscous Salad

Couscous is made from semolina which has been cracked. When cooked, it is similar to teeny tiny grains of rice. In this recipe, marinated vegetables are spooned into the centre of a bed of couscous. This recipe makes a colourful side-dish salad.

285g/10 oz couscous

1 tin (395g/14 oz) chicken broth

225g/8 oz broccoli florets

140g/5 oz diagonally sliced carrots

200ml/7 fl oz vegetable oil

90ml/3 fl oz red wine vinegar

2 tablespoons freshly squeezed lemon juice

2 tablespoons Dijon-style mustard

1 tablespoon finely chopped fresh basil or 1 teaspoon dried basil leaves, crushed

1 medium garlic clove, cut in half

1/8 teaspoon freshly ground black pepper

1 tin (425g/15 oz) chick peas, drained

1 medium courgette, diagonally sliced

1 medium yellow squash, diagonally sliced

1 medium red onion, coarsely chopped

1 medium red pepper, cored, seeded, and cut into 2cm/1-inch pieces

Place the couscous in a large heatproof bowl. In a medium-size saucepan, over high heat, bring the chicken broth to a boil. Pour the chicken broth over the couscous, stir and cover. Stand for 10 minutes so that the couscous absorbs the broth. Fluff the couscous with a fork.

Meanwhile, bring a large saucepan of water to the boil. Add the broccoli and carrots and cook for 1 minute. Rinse the broccoli and carrots under cold water and drain well.

In another large bowl, stir together the oil, vinegar, lemon juice, mustard, basil, garlic and pepper. Add the broccoli, carrots, chick peas, courgettes, yellow squash, red onion, and red pepper and toss to coat with the dressing.

Spread the couscous on a serving dish, building up the edges slightly. Top with the vegetables. Remove the garlic halves before serving.

Makes 6 servings.

She Gets a Hen Party and Twenty-Seven Gifts … I Get Asked to Bring Food Brown and Wild Rice Salad with Carrots and Dried Cranberries

Serve this salad in a large bowl that is lined with green leaf lettuce. Turn the salad into the main event by adding 285g/10 oz bite-size pieces of cooked chicken.

740ml/26 fl oz water

1 1/2 teaspoons salt

200g/7 oz uncooked brown rice

115g/4 oz wild rice, rinsed and drained

90ml/3 fl oz vegetable oil

3 tablespoons red wine vinegar

1 tablespoon freshly squeezed lemon juice

1 tablespoon Dijon-style mustard

1 medium garlic clove, finely chopped

1/4 teaspoon Tabasco pepper sauce

140g/5 oz dried cranberries

170g/6 oz grated carrots

45g/1 1/2 oz sliced spring onions (including tender green tops)

55g/2 oz coarsely broken toasted pecans (optional, see Note)

In a heavy large saucepan, bring the water and salt to a boil. Stir in the brown and wild rice and return the mixture to the boil. Reduce the heat, cover, and simmer for 50 to 60 minutes, or until the rice is tender and the water is completely absorbed.

Meanwhile, in a large bowl, stir together the oil, vinegar, lemon juice, mustard, garlic and Tabasco pepper sauce. Add the cooked rice and cranberries and let the mixture cool.

Stir in the carrots and spring onions. Let the mixture stand at least 2 hours or refrigerate overnight to allow the flavours to blend. Before serving, return to room temperature, adjust seasonings if necessary, and sprinkle the surface with the pecans, if desired.

Makes 6 to 8 servings.

Note: To toast the nuts, place them in a single layer on a baking sheet and bake in a preheated oven at 180°C/350°F/Gas Mark 4 for 5 to 7 minutes, shaking the sheet a couple of times, until the nuts are lightly browned.

No, I Did NOT Buy This at a Deli and Throw Out the Container **Potato Green Bean Salad**

Bring this sturdy salad to your next picnic. Make it the day before to allow the flavours to blend.

1.3kg/3 lb small potatoes, scrubbed and trimmed of blemishes

$2^1/_2$ teaspoons salt

455g/1 lb green beans, trimmed and cut into 4cm/$1^1/_2$ inch pieces

4 tablespoons olive oil

4 tablespoons balsamic vinegar

2 tablespoons freshly squeezed lemon juice

2 tablespoons Dijon-style mustard

1 teaspoon finely chopped garlic

$^1/_4$ teaspoon freshly ground pepper

15g/$^1/_2$ oz chopped fresh parsley (optional)

Place the potatoes in a large saucepan and add enough water to cover. Add 1 tea-spoon of the salt. Cover the pan and bring the water to the boil. Reduce the heat and keep at a low boil for 30 to 40 minutes, or until the potatoes are tender when pierced with a fork. Thoroughly drain the potatoes. Cut the potatoes into 4cm/1^1/$_2$ inch chunks.

Place the green beans in a large pan. Add enough water to cover and 1 teaspoon of the salt. Cover and bring the mixture to the boil. Reduce the heat and simmer for 7 to 9 minutes, or until the beans are crisp-tender. Thoroughly drain.

Meanwhile, in a large bowl, stir together the oil, vinegar, lemon juice, mustard, garlic, remaining 1/2 teaspoon of salt and pepper to make the dressing.

Add the warm cooked vegetables to the dressing and toss gently to combine. Cover and refrigerate, tossing gently occasionally. Just before serving, sprinkle with the chopped parsley, if desired.

Makes 6 to 8 servings.

Why Did I Volunteer to Bring Something
Party Pasta Salad

When it's time to create an easy dish to feed the masses, a pasta salad is hard to beat. This recipe idea could be scaled down to serve a single. Next time you cook pasta for dinner, make a little extra to use in a salad the next day. Make sure you cook the pasta in water that has been salted so it does not taste flat.

455g/1 lb pasta shapes

340ml/12 fl oz regular or reduced-calorie mayonnaise

90ml/3 fl oz red wine vinegar

3 tablespoons freshly squeezed lemon juice

1 tablespoon Dijon-style mustard

1 teaspoon salt

1/2 teaspoon dried basil leaves, crushed

1/2 teaspoon dried oregano leaves, crushed

1/4 teaspoon Tabasco pepper sauce

455g/1 lb cooked prawns (see Note)

1 medium red pepper, seeded and chopped

1 medium tomato, chopped

115g/4 oz chopped stoned ripe olives

30g/1 oz chopped fresh parsley

Cook the pasta according to the instructions in lightly salted water. Rinse with cold water and drain thoroughly.

Meanwhile, in a large bowl, stir together the mayonnaise, vinegar, lemon juice, mustard, salt, basil, oregano and Tabasco. Add the pasta, prawns, pepper, tomato, olives and parsley, and toss gently to coat the ingredients with the dressing. Cover and refrigerate for at least one hour. Toss the salad gently, taste, and adjust the seasonings.

Makes about 8 servings.

Note: Other types of cooked seafood, chicken, or turkey could be used in place of the prawns. For instance, substitute 2 tins (170g/6 oz) tuna, drained and flaked, for the prawns. Cooked, tinned or frozen crabmeat is also delicious.

Keep Them Eating and They Won't Have Time to Look in My Bathroom Cabinets
Apple Cranberry Crisp

This is wonderful topped with a big scoop of vanilla ice cream or whipped cream. You can trim off the peel of the apples if you'd like, but it is also delicious with the peel on. Try other fruits baked underneath this delicious topping mixture.

4 medium tart apples (such as Granny Smith), cored and sliced

140g/5 oz fresh or thawed frozen cranberries

115g/4 oz brown sugar

55g/2 oz plain flour

55g/2 oz old-fashioned rolled oats

85g/3 oz unsalted butter, softened

3/4 teaspoon ground cinnamon

1/4 teaspoon ground ginger

Preheat the oven to 190°C/375°F/Gas Mark 5. Lightly grease the base and sides of a 20–23cm/8 or 9 inch square baking tin.

Toss the apple slices and cranberries together in the prepared tin.

In a medium bowl, stir together the brown sugar, flour, oats, butter, cinnamon and ginger and sprinkle the mixture over the fruit. Bake for 25 to 30 minutes, or until the topping is lightly browned and the fruits are tender. It is best served warm.

Makes 6 servings.

I'll Need at Least Three Hours to Prepare My Casual, Carefree Look, so I'd Better Get Started
Make-Ahead Ziti Bake

Here's a hearty Italian-style dish that you can make ahead of time. Offer balsamic vinegar and extra-virgin olive oil as accompaniments for dipping hearty wholegrain bread into. Serve with a tossed salad to fill out the meal.

455g/1 lb ziti or other pasta shapes

2 tablespoons olive oil

225g/8 oz chopped onions

4 medium garlic cloves, finely chopped

1 tablespoon dried basil leaves, crushed

1/2 teaspoon crushed red pepper flakes

1/4 teaspoon dried oregano leaves, crushed

5 tins (400g/14 oz) Italian-style plum tomatoes, drained and chopped

1 tin (225g/8 oz) tomato sauce

4 tablespoons tomato purée

455g/1 lb mozzarella cheese, grated

55g/2 oz freshly grated Parmesan cheese

HOSTESS WITH THE MOSTEST

PANIC   INSECURITY

ANXIETY   GUILT

Cook the pasta according to the instructions and drain thoroughly.

In a large heavy saucepan, heat the oil over medium heat. Add the onions, garlic, basil, red pepper flakes and oregano. Cook for about 5 to 7 minutes, or until the vegetables are softened, stirring occasionally.

Stir in the chopped tomatoes, tomato sauce and tomato purée. Simmer, uncovered, for 30 to 40 minutes, or until the mixture has thickened slightly, stirring occasionally.

Preheat the oven to 180°C/350°F/Gas Mark 4.

In a large bowl combine the cooked pasta, tomato sauce, half of the mozzarella cheese, and the Parmesan cheese. Place the mixture in a large baking dish (approximately 33 × 23 × 5cm/13 × 9 × 2 inches). Cover the dish with tin foil and bake for 20 minutes. Uncover and sprinkle the surface evenly with the remaining mozzarella cheese. Bake for 10 minutes longer, or until the cheese is melted.

Makes 8 to 10 servings.

Note: This dish can be prepared up to 2 days ahead. Before sprinkling the mozzarella cheese on top, cover and refrigerate the pasta mixture. When ready to serve, bake the pasta mixture, covered, for 40 to 50 minutes, or until the mixture is heated through. Sprinkle the surface evenly with the remaining mozzarella cheese and bake for 10 minutes longer.

Oh No, He Invited His Mother
Fillet of Beef with Horseradish Sauce

If you start with one of the most tender cuts of meat (at a price, of course), it's difficult to mess it up. Fillet of beef is delicious served hot or at room temperature, so the pressure is off to get everything done at the same time. It is great served as part of a buffet. Allow about 225g/8 oz raw fillet per person.

Fillet of Beef:

1 fillet of beef (at least 2.7kg/6 lb)

6 strips of bacon

Salt and freshly ground black pepper to taste

Horseradish Sauce:

120ml/4 fl oz double or whipping cream, chilled

15g/$^1/_2$ oz prepared horseradish, drained

120ml/4 fl oz mayonnaise

2 tablespoons Dijon-style mustard

$^1/_4$ teaspoon Tabasco pepper sauce

To make the fillet of beef:
With a sharp, pointed knife, trim the fat and thin fibrous covering from the fillet. Tuck the thin tail end under the fillet and secure it with a string. Let the fillet stand at room temperature for about 1 hour before cooking.

Preheat the oven to its highest setting. Place the fillet on a rack in a roasting tin and lay the strips of bacon over the meat. Reduce the heat immediately to 200°C/400°F/Gas Mark 4 and bake for about 30 minutes. (The fillet is rare when the internal temperature is 120 to 125°F on a meat thermometer. For medium rare, cook for 130 to 140°F. For medium, cook to 145 to 150°F. For well done, cook to 155 to 165°F.) Remove the bacon and continue cooking the bacon longer, if desired, to serve it alongside the fillet. Cut the meat into 1.5 to 2cm/^{1}/$_2$ to ^{3}/$_4$ thick slices.

To make the horseradish sauce:
In a chilled medium bowl, using a handheld electric mixer with chilled beaters set at medium-high speed, beat the cream until peaks just start to form.

In a large bowl, stir together the horseradish, mayonnaise, mustard and Tabasco pepper sauce. Using a rubber spatula, gently fold one-third of the whipped cream into the horseradish mixture to lighten it. Fold in the remaining whipped cream until just combined. Serve with the sliced fillet and bacon.

Makes at least 18 servings (if you allow about 140g/5 oz cooked meat per person).

I'm Sure Someone Was Born Today
Chocolate Chip Birthday Cake

This delicious two-layer cake could give you a reputation as baker extraordinaire. It's easy and much more 'natural' than making a cake mix or serving a shop-bought cake. This dense white cake is full of chocolate chips and then the whole shebang is coated with a rich chocolatey icing.

Cake:

255g/9oz chocolate chips

395g/14oz plain flour, divided

2 teaspoons baking powder

$^1/_2$ teaspoon salt

225g/8oz unsalted butter or margarine, softened

340g/12oz granulated sugar

4 large eggs, at room temperature

2 teaspoons vanilla essence

285ml/$^1/_2$ pint milk, at room temperature

Chocolate Icing:

455g/1lb chocolate flavoured icing sugar

115g/4oz butter or margarine, softened

90ml/3floz milk

1 teaspoon vanilla essence

To make the cake:
Preheat the oven to 180°C/350°F/Gas Mark 4. Lightly grease two 20cm/9 inch round cake tins. Dust the tins with flour and lightly tap them to shake out the excess flour.

In a medium bowl, stir together the chocolate chips and 2 tablespoons of the flour until combined. (This will prevent the chocolate chips from settling to the bottom.)

In a large bowl, stir together the remaining flour, baking powder, and salt.

In another large bowl with an electric mixer set on high speed, beat the butter and sugar for about 2 minutes until well blended. One at a time, beat in the eggs, beating well after each addition. Beat in the vanilla essence.

With the mixer set on low speed, in three additions each, alternately beat in the flour mixture and the milk, scraping the side of the bowl as necessary. Beat until the ingredients are just incorporated. Using a wooden spoon, stir in the chocolate chips.

Divide the batter evenly between the prepared tins and smooth the surface. Bake for 30 to 35 minutes, or until a skewer inserted into the centre of each cake comes out clean. Cool the cakes in the tins set on a wire rack for 15 minutes. Carefully remove the cakes from the tins and cool completely on the wire rack.

Makes 12 to 14 servings.

To make the chocolate icing:
In a large bowl, with an electric mixer set on high speed, beat the icing sugar, butter, milk and vanilla until smooth, adding a small amount of milk if necessary to achieve spreading consistency.

Place one cake layer on a serving platter. Spread about 200ml/7 fl oz icing. Place the second cake layer on top. Ice the side and then the top of the cake.

Consolation Food

Consolation Food

I've never met a man who understood me as well as a chocolate chip cookie, and in a way, I hope I never do.

When I'm miserable, I don't want empathetic dialogue. I want food. Food like my mum used to make for me. Food like my mum would still make for me if I were willing to invite her over, tell her everything, and listen to her advice.

I want to act like a five-year-old, sound like a five-year-old, and eat like a five-year-old. I want food that hugs me inside and out. Food that says, 'Plbttt!!' to the rest of the world. Food that instantly re-creates that beautiful, perfect time of life when I believed with all my heart that the entire universe revolved around me.

I want food that restores my confidence, my sense of justice, my equilibrium, my perspective, and my sense of humour.

You just can't stay that fed up for that long with a spoonful of really, really good mashed potatoes in your mouth.

The Proposal Is Due; I Lost the File; I'm Staying Home Chicken Noodle Soup

There seems to be a secret ingredient in chicken soup that is good for whatever ails you.

1 tablespoon olive oil

115g/4 oz chopped onion

115g/4 oz chopped celery

1 medium garlic clove, finely chopped

850ml/1 1/2 pints chicken broth or stock

1 tin (455g/1 lb) whole tomatoes, undrained and cut up

285g/10 oz frozen mixed vegetables

1 teaspoon dried basil leaves, crushed

1 medium bay leaf

85g/3 oz medium egg noodles

285g/10 oz bite-size pieces of cooked chicken

Salt and pepper to taste

In a large saucepan, heat the oil over medium heat. Add the onion, celery and garlic and cook, stirring frequently, for 5 to 7 minutes, or until the vegetables are tender.

Add the chicken broth, tomatoes and juice, vegetables, basil and bay leaf. Bring the mixture to the boil. Stir in the noodles and cook for 7 minutes longer. Add the chicken and continue cooking until the mixture is heated through. Remove the bay leaf before serving. Season with salt and pepper. Serve in warmed mugs or bowls.

Makes about 4 to 6 servings.

My Favourite Soap Was Cancelled and Replaced by Football Highlights Toasted Cheese Sandwich

Of course, for ultimate comfort, you can have one of these soul-satisfying sandwiches with a mug of tomato soup. While the classic combo is Cheddar cheese and white bread, try other varieties of cheese. For instance, Brie is a sophisticated filling with hearty wholegrain bread. Add a slice of ham if you like. If your butter is straight from the fridge, soften it by putting it in a small microwave-safe dish in the microwave oven. Put the microwave on the defrost setting and defrost for 20 to 30 seconds until the butter is of spreading consistency.

2 to 3 teaspoons butter, softened

2 slices of bread

2 to 3 slices of cheese

Spread half of the butter on one side of each piece of bread. Place the cheese in between the bread slices, with the buttered sides facing out. Heat a nonstick pan or frying pan over medium-high heat. Place the sandwich in the pan and cook for 2 to 3 minutes on each side, or until lightly browned.

Makes 1 serving.

BAD HAIR
BAD FACE
BAD BODY
AND
BAD BRAIN
DAY

The Boy I Dumped in Primary School Just Purchased Asia **Macaroni Cheese**

If you like macaroni cheese that is a little soupier, add an extra 4 tablespoons of milk.

225g/8 oz macaroni

1 tablespoon butter

1 tablespoon plain flour

1/4 teaspoon dry mustard

Dash of ground pepper

340ml/12 fl oz milk

225g/8 oz pasteurized processed cheese spread, cut into 1.5cm/1/2-inch pieces

Preheat the oven to 180°C/350°F/Gas Mark 4. Cook the macaroni according to the instructions and drain thoroughly.

In a large saucepan, melt the butter over medium heat. Stir in the flour, mustard and pepper and cook, stirring constantly until combined. Gradually stir in the milk and continue to cook, stirring frequently, until the mixture is hot. Add the cheese spread and continue cooking and stirring until the cheese spread has melted. Remove the pan from the heat and stir in the macaroni until just combined. Scrape the mixture into an ovenproof baking dish. Bake for 25 minutes, or until bubbly.

Makes 4 servings.

My Credit Card Bill Just Arrived
Tuna Noodle Casserole

When it comes to comfort, sometimes nothing else will do than this easy tried-and-true classic. If your guy is a classic kind of guy, you might want to file this under the Romance chapter!

115g/4 oz medium noodles or macaroni

1 tablespoon butter

55g/2 oz chopped onion

1 tin (285g/10 oz) condensed cream of mushroom soup

200ml/7 fl oz milk

1 tin (200g/7 oz) tuna, drained and flaked

140g/5 oz frozen peas or frozen peas and carrots

1 bag crushed potato crisps (optional)

Preheat the oven to 200°C/400°F/Gas Mark 6. Cook the noodles or macaroni according to the instructions and drain thoroughly.

In a large saucepan, melt the butter over medium heat. Add the onion and cook, stirring frequently, for 4 to 6 minutes, or until the onion is tender.

Stir in the soup, milk, tuna and vegetables until just mixed. Stir in the noodles until combined. Scrape the mixture into an ovenproof baking dish. Bake for 20 minutes, or until heated through. If desired, sprinkle with the crushed potato crisps and bake 5 minutes longer.

Makes 4 servings.

Does Everyone Drive Like an Idiot
Chicken Pot Pie

Frozen puff pastry makes a delectable topping for this homey chicken pot pie.

2 tablespoons butter

115g/4 oz chopped onion

55g/2 oz plain flour

1 teaspoon fresh marjoram leaves, chopped or 1/2 teaspoon dried marjoram leaves, crushed

340ml/12 fl oz milk

340ml/12 fl oz chicken broth or stock

425g/15 oz bite-size pieces of cooked chicken

285g/10 oz frozen peas and carrots

15g/1/2 oz chopped fresh parsley

Salt and ground white pepper to taste

455g/1 lb frozen puff pastry, thawed according to package directions

1 egg yolk mixed with 1 teaspoon water (for the egg wash)

Preheat the oven to 200°C/400°F/Gas Mark 6.

In a large saucepan, melt the butter over medium heat. Add the onion and cook, stirring frequently, for 4 to 6 minutes, or until the onion is tender. Stir in the flour and marjoram. Add the milk and broth and continue cooking, stirring constantly, for about 5 minutes, or until the sauce thickens slightly. Stir in the chicken, peas and carrots and parsley. Season with salt and pepper and continue cooking until the mixture is hot. Spoon the chicken mixture into a baking dish.

Place the pastry loosely over the filling in the baking dish. Trim the edge of the pastry, leaving a 2cm/1-inch overhang. Brush the top surface of the pastry with the egg wash. Bake for 15 to 20 minutes, or until the pastry is golden brown. (To eliminate spills onto the bottom of your oven place the dish on a baking sheet.)

Makes 4 servings.

I Want to Go Home But I Don't Want to Live There **Meatloaf**

Here's a delicious meatloaf that is chock full of mushrooms! Make sure to save some for a leftover meatloaf sandwich or two.

2 teaspoons vegetable oil

170g/6 oz sliced mushrooms

1 medium onion, chopped

680g/1 1/2 lb ground beef

85g/3 oz Italian-seasoned dry breadcrumbs

2 large eggs

2 tablespoons Dijon-style mustard

1/4 teaspoon freshly ground black pepper

1 teaspoon prepared horseradish

Preheat the oven to 180°C/350°F/Gas Mark 4. In a large skillet or frying pan, heat the oil over medium heat. Add the mushrooms and onion and cook, stirring occasionally, for 8 to 10 minutes, or until the vegetables are softened. Remove the pan from the heat.

In a large bowl, using your hands or a wooden spoon, mix the cooked vegetables and the remaining ingredients until well combined.

Spoon the mixture into an ovenproof glass loaf tin (approximately 23 x 13 x 8cm/9 x 5 x 3 inches) and smooth the surface. Bake for 1 hour, or until cooked through and no longer pink in the centre. Loosen the loaf from the tin and drain off the drippings. Invert the meatloaf onto a warmed serving platter. Let stand for 5 minutes before cutting into slices to serve.

Makes 6 servings.

Who Needs Him Anyway
Mashed Potatoes

When it comes to comfort, there is nothing like a big bowl of mashed potatoes to soothe the soul. While many people like their mashed potatoes left unadulterated, try stirring in a small amount of one or more of the following to add extra interest: grated Parmesan, Cheddar, or another type of cheese; chopped spring onions or red onions; chopped, drained, sun-dried tomatoes; or chopped raw or cooked garlic. Use a potato masher instead of an electric mixer to work out a lot of anxiety.

6 medium potatoes, scrubbed

1 teaspoon salt plus additional salt to taste

55g/2 oz butter, softened

Ground white pepper to taste

About 6 tablespoons hot milk

In a large saucepan, combine the potatoes, enough water to cover, and 1 teaspoon of the salt. Cover the pan and bring the mixture to the boil and cook for 30 to 35 minutes, or until the potatoes are tender. Drain and peel the potatoes. (You can trim off the blemishes and leave on all or some of the skin if you like for a little extra texture.) Return the potatoes to the pan.

Using a handheld electric mixer or a potato masher, beat the potatoes with the butter until combined. Season with salt and pepper. Gradually add 4 tablespoons of the hot milk and beat. Beat in more milk if necessary to create potatoes that are light and fluffy. Do not overbeat. Serve immediately or scrape the potatoes into a buttered casserole and keep warm in a low oven.

Makes about 4 to 6 servings.

My Make-Over Took Seven Hours
Hot Fudge Sauce

This multi-purpose sauce can be poured over whatever you want – cake, ice cream, brownie sundaes, etc. If you like, you can add a tablespoon of your favourite liqueur (such as cognac or Grand Marnier) along with the vanilla. Basically it is a ganache (a mixture of double cream and chocolate). If you freeze the mixture, it can then be shaped into small (about 1 to 2 teaspoons) balls to form the base for truffles. After you form the balls, roll them into finely chopped nuts. Freeze the truffles for up to one month. Thaw slightly before serving.

140ml/5 fl oz double cream

1 1/2 teaspoons unsalted butter

A few grains of salt

3/4 teaspoon instant espresso or coffee powder

170g/6 oz plain chocolate, finely chopped

1 teaspoon vanilla essence

In a heavy, small saucepan, combine the cream, butter and salt. Slowly bring the mixture to a gentle boil over medium-low heat. Remove the pan from the heat. Stir in the espresso powder. Whisk in the chocolate until smooth. Stir in the vanilla.

Makes about 340ml/12 fl oz sauce.

I Really, Really, Really Deserve a Raise
Doughnuts

Homemade doughnuts are a little more work than driving to the local doughnut shop. However, once you get the hang of them, you'll probably want to make them over and over again. Plus when you make them at home, you don't have to put on your makeup for the doughnut man (or order an embarrassingly large number of doughnuts for yourself). To transfer the doughnuts for frying without stretching them out of shape, dip a metal pancake turner into the hot oil. Pick up the doughnuts and they will slide right off!

455g/1 lb plain flour

2 teaspoons baking powder

1 teaspoon bicarbonate of soda

1 teaspoon ground cinnamon

1/2 teaspoon ground ginger

1/2 teaspoon salt

2 large eggs

200g/7 oz granulated sugar plus extra for coating (optional)

140ml/5 fl oz buttermilk or milk

55g/2 oz unsalted butter, melted

1 1/2 teaspoons vanilla essence

Vegetable oil for deep-fat frying

Icing sugar, cinnamon sugar or Chocolate Glaze (recipe follows) for coating (optional)

In a large bowl, sift together the flour, baking powder, bicarbonate of soda, cinnamon, ginger and salt.

In another large bowl, using a handheld electric mixer set at medium-high speed, beat the eggs and granulated sugar until combined. In a small bowl, stir together the buttermilk, butter and vanilla until combined. Beat this mixture into the egg mixture. With the mixer set on low speed, add the flour mixture and beat just until smooth. Cover the dough and refrigerate it for about 1 hour.

In a deep-fat fryer or a heavy saucepan, heat the oil to 190°C/375°F.

While the oil is heating, cut out the doughnuts. On a well-floured work surface, with a floured rolling pin or floured hands, roll or pat the dough out so it is about 1.5cm/1 inch thick. With a floured doughnut cutter, cut out the doughnuts and doughnut holes. Gather the scraps together and reroll and cut out the doughnuts and holes until all the dough is used.

Add the doughnuts to the oil, three at a time, and cook for about 30 to 60 seconds on each side, or until golden, turning once with a slotted spoon. Lift the doughnuts from the hot oil with the slotted spoon and drain the doughnuts on several layers of paper towels. Repeat with the remaining doughnuts and doughnut holes (cooking about eight of the holes together at a time). Serve them as they are, or shake them in a bag with granulated, icing or cinnamon sugar, or dip or drizzle the tops with Chocolate Glaze, if desired.

Makes about 16 doughnuts.

Chocolate Glaze

Great for dunking Doughnuts (page 124) into, this also makes a decadent glaze or drizzle for cakes. Sprinkle a few chopped nuts, coloured sprinkles, or toasted coconut on top of the glaze for extra decadence.

115g/4 oz plain or milk chocolate

3 tablespoons unsalted butter

1/2 teaspoon vanilla essence

225g/8 oz sifted icing sugar

2 to 4 tablespoons hot water

In a large microwave-safe bowl, heat the chocolate and butter in a microwave oven on high for 1 to 3 minutes, stirring halfway through cooking, until the chocolate is melted (or use a bowl over hot, not simmering, water). Whisk in the vanilla. Whisk in the icing sugar. Whisk in enough hot water to make the glaze of the right consistency for either dunking doughnuts or drizzling over cakes.

Makes about 340ml/12 fl oz glaze.

I've Been Waiting for His 'I'll Call You' for the Last Twelve Days Colossal Chocolate Chip Peanut Butter Cookies

If you only want to eat one cookie, this is the one to go for. Each cookie measures about 13cm/5 inches across. They freeze well.

285g/10 oz plain flour

170g/6 oz rolled oats

1 teaspoon baking powder

1 teaspoon bicarbonate of soda

1/2 teaspoon salt

225g/8 oz unsalted butter, softened

455g/1 lb crunchy peanut butter

395g/14 oz brown sugar

2 large eggs, at room temperature

1 tablespoon vanilla essence

340g/12 oz chocolate chips

Stir together the flour, oats, baking powder, bicarbonate of soda and salt. In another bowl, cream together the butter, peanut butter and sugar. Add the eggs, stirring well after each addition. Stir in the vanilla. Gradually stir in the flour mixture until combined, and the chocolate. Cover and refrigerate the dough for at least 2 hours or overnight.

Preheat the oven to 150°C/300°F/Gas Mark 2. Position one oven rack in the top one-third of the oven and the other oven rack in the bottom third of the oven. Using a 1/2-cup measuring cup, drop the dough onto baking sheets, about 8cm/3 inches between cookies. Flatten each mound slightly. Bake for 40 to 45 minutes, switching the positions of the baking sheets halfway through, until the cookies are lightly golden. Remove the baking sheets to wire racks and cool for 5 minutes. Using a metal spatula, transfer the cookies to wire racks and cool completely. Repeat until all the dough is used. When cool, store the cookies in an airtight container for up to 2 weeks. These cookies freeze well for up to 3 months.

Makes about 14 jumbo cookies.

I Swear I'll Never Buy Anything Else
Chocolate Chip Cookies (or Dough)

This cookie dough freezes well. For future snacking, package the dough into portion-controlled servings and store it in the freezer for up to 3 months.

310g/11 oz plain flour

3/4 teaspoon baking powder

1/4 teaspoon salt

225g/8 oz unsalted butter, softened

170g/6 oz dark brown sugar

85g/3 oz granulated sugar

2 large eggs, at room temperature

2 teaspoons vanilla essence

340g/12 oz chocolate chips

115g/4 oz chopped walnuts or pecans

In a large bowl, stir together the flour, baking powder, and salt. In another bowl, using a wooden spoon, cream together the butter and sugars. One at a time, add the eggs, stirring well after each addition. Stir in the vanilla. Gradually stir in the flour mixture until combined. Stir in the chocolate chips and nuts. Eat the dough. (See Note below).

Chocolate Chip Cookie Variation:
Cover and refrigerate the dough (any that is left over) for at least 2 hours or overnight.

Preheat the oven to 180°C/350°F/Gas Mark 4. Drop the dough by rounded table-spoonfuls onto an ungreased baking sheet, leaving 3cm/2 inches between the dough mounds. Bake for 10 to 13 minutes, or until the cookies are lightly browned. Remove the baking sheet to a wire rack and cool for 5 minutes. Using a metal spatula, transfer the cookies to wire racks and cool completely. Repeat until all the dough is used. When cool, store the cookies in an airtight container for up to 2 weeks.

These cookies freeze well for up to 3 months.

If all the dough turns into cookies, you should get about 50 cookies.

Note: If you are concerned about salmonella from eating raw eggs, use a pasteurized egg product instead of the 2 eggs.

I Want Comfort and I Want It Now
Fast Fudge

This easy fudge recipe is made with cream cheese as its base so there is no need to hassle with a sugar thermometer.

225g/8 oz cream cheese, softened

225g/8 oz chocolate, melted and cooled

1 teaspoon vanilla essence

115g/4 oz chopped walnuts or pecans

Lightly grease a 20cm/8-inch-square tin.

In a large bowl, using a handheld electric mixer, beat the cream cheese just until it is smooth. Beat in the melted chocolate and vanilla. Using a wooden spoon, stir in the nuts.

Scrape the batter into the prepared tin and spread evenly. Cover and refrigerate the fudge until it is firm. Cut into 2.5cm/1-inch squares. Store in an airtight container in the refrigerator for up to 2 weeks.

Makes about 64 squares.

I Think I'm Going Insane **Peanut Butter Squares**

Peanuts and chocolate are a great flavour combination.

85g/3 oz white chocolate, broken into pieces

170g/6 oz crunchy peanut butter

115g/4 oz icing sugar

1 tablespoon vanilla essence

85g/3 oz plain chocolate, broken into pieces

Lightly grease a 20cm/8-inch-square baking tin.

In a microwave-safe bowl, heat the white chocolate on high for 1 to 2 minutes, stirring halfway through cooking, until the chocolate is melted (or use a bowl over hot, not simmering, water). Stir in the peanut butter, icing sugar and vanilla, until combined. Scrape the mixture into the prepared tin and spread it into an even layer.

In a microwave-safe bowl, heat the plain chocolate on high for 1 to 2 minutes, stirring halfway through cooking, until the chocolate is melted (or use a bowl over hot, not simmering, water). Quickly pour the chocolate over the peanut butter and spread it evenly over the surface. Refrigerate until set. Cut into 2.5cm/1-inch squares. (If it is difficult to make even cuts through the chocolate, let the tin stand at room temperature before cutting into squares.)

Makes about 64 squares.

My Hair Dryer Just Broke and I Can't Leave the House Ice Cream Pie

The base of this pie is basically a jumbo chocolate chip cookie. Topped with ice cream, it is a decadent combination of two consolation foods.

170g/6 oz plain flour

1/2 teaspoon baking powder

1/4 teaspoon salt

115g/4 oz unsalted butter, softened

115g/4 oz brown sugar

55g/2 oz granulated sugar

1 large egg, at room temperature

1 teaspoon vanilla essence

170g/6 oz chocolate chips

1.2 litres/2 pints ice cream

Sweetened whipped cream, chocolate shavings, or Hot Fudge Sauce (page 123) for topping (optional)

Preheat the oven to 190°C/375°F/Gas Mark 5. Generously butter a 23cm/9 inch ovenproof pie dish. In a large bowl, stir together the flour, baking powder and salt. In another bowl, cream together the butter and sugars. Add the egg, stirring well. Stir in the vanilla. Gradually stir in the flour mixture until combined. Stir in the chocolate chips.

Scrape the batter into the prepared pie dish and smooth the surface evenly. Bake for 25 to 30 minutes, or until it is lightly golden and a skewer inserted into the centre comes out clean. Set on a wire rack and cool the cookie crust in the dish.

When the crust is completely cooled, let the ice cream stand at room temperature for 10 to 15 minutes, or until it is softened slightly. Mound the ice cream on top of the crust and smooth the surface. Cover the pie loosely with clingfilm and freeze for at least 4 hours, or until the ice cream is firm enough to cut into wedges. Top the pie with sweetened whipped cream, chocolate shavings, or Hot Fudge Sauce.

Makes 8 servings.

I'm Turning into My Mother Anyway, So Why Not Eat Some Chocolate Pudding

When you are looking for an intense chocolate experience and the satisfaction of smooth and creamy pudding, here's the recipe to go for. Plain chocolate adds extra chocolate flavour to the smooth and delicious pudding.

200g/7 oz granulated sugar

55g/2 oz cornflour

Pinch of salt

3 large egg yolks, lightly beaten

850ml/1 1/2 pints milk

225g/8 oz plain chocolate, finely chopped

2 teaspoons vanilla essence

In a large heavy saucepan, stir together the sugar, cornflour and salt. Gradually whisk in the egg yolks until they are combined. Gradually whisk in the milk.

Cook the mixture over medium heat, stirring constantly with a whisk, for about 10 minutes, or until the mixture thickens and comes to the boil. Remove the pan from the heat and whisk in the chocolate and vanilla, whisking until smooth. Quickly pour the mixture through a strainer into a bowl. Serve at once or cover the surface of the pudding with a piece of clingfilm to prevent a 'skin' from forming. Refrigerate any leftover pudding.

Makes a bit more than 1.2 litres/2 pints of pudding; servings vary according to the comfort needs of the consumer.

Index

Index